U . GR

INTRODUCTION TO JUDAISM

FOR HARVEY AND FRANCINE

INTRODUCTION
TO
JUDAISM

by
ISIDORE FISHMAN
M.A., Ph.D.

JEWISH CHRONICLE PUBLICATIONS

Published by
JEWISH CHRONICLE PUBLICATIONS
25 Furnival Street, London EC4A 1JT
© Isidore Fishman

ISBN 0 85303 091 X

First Impression 1958
Second Impression (Revised) 1959
Third Impression 1962
Fourth Impression 1964
Fifth Impression 1966
Sixth Impression 1969
Seventh Impression (Revised) 1970
Eighth Impression 1973
Ninth Impression 1978
Eleventh Impression 1982

Printed in Great Britain by The Furnival Press, London SE5 9HR

CONTENTS

CONTENTS

PREFACE

This book is intended to be an introduction to the beliefs, practices and ethical teachings of traditional Judaism. Although much has been written on this subject, I have felt that there is still a need to provide young people with a simple exposition.

The Torah, the inspiration of the Jewish way of life, guides our daily thought and conduct. So a special section of the book is devoted to its ethical and moral teachings, showing the Jewish attitude to current social problems.

I hope my modest effort will encourage the reader to seek a deeper knowledge of the Jewish Faith through studying the original Biblical and Rabbinic sources on which it is based.

Isidore Fishman

THE BEGINNING OF KNOWLEDGE

Jewish teachers and scholars have never tired of bidding their people acquire knowledge as one of the chief aims in life. The Book of Proverbs (i, 7) tells us that *the fear of the Lord is the beginning of knowledge*. Belief in God, approaching Him with reverence—this is the starting point of all the theory and practice of Judaism.

1 God the Creator

In the beginning God created the heaven and the earth.

The first verse of the Bible clearly declares one of the main principles of our Faith. God was the Creator and first Cause of all things. He brought the World into existence: fashioning it out of nothing, getting order and perfection out of chaos. Taking the first word of the Bible '*Bereshith*,' which begins with the letter *beth* (representing *berachah*—blessing), the Rabbis comment that the universe was created for the blessing of its inhabitants (*Bereshith Rabbah* i, 14).

It is not possible for the human mind to grasp the idea of creation out of nothing. The Jewish belief is that the universe has not existed for all eternity, and that an Eternal and Supreme Being apart from it, yet greater than it, guides our daily life and actions, and is personally concerned with our well-being.

When other people have questioned this belief in God's

existence, Jewish scholars and philosophers have tried to convince them. The Emperor Hadrian, the Talmud tells us, once said to Rabbi Joshua ben Chananya, 'I wish to see your God.' 'That is impossible,' was the reply, but the Emperor persisted, 'I wish to see Him.' It was during the month of *Tammuz*, the hottest period of the year. Rabbi Joshua asked the Emperor to face the sun: 'Look up at it!' 'It is impossible to do so,' he answered. Said the Rabbi: 'If you admit you can't gaze at the sun, which is only one of the attendants standing before the Holy One, how much more beyond your power must it be to look at the Divine Presence!' (*Chullin* 59 b).

One of the arguments of thinkers is this: The mysterious workings of nature, controlled in an orderly pattern, and each serving a specific purpose for the benefit of the human race, testify to the existence of a Supreme Being. Others base the knowledge of God on the actual experiences of Israel, such as the Divine Deliverance from Egypt and the Revelation at Mount Sinai. Then there is the evidence of the Jews' miraculous preservation in the face of innumerable attempts by other nations to destroy them.

But although the study of nature, human experience and history may lead us to recognise that there is a Divine Power and Providence, the chief pillar of our belief in the existence of an Almighty Being is Faith.

2 The Unity of God

Hear, O Israel, the Lord our God, the Lord is One (*Deut.* vi, 4).

Commenting on these words our Rabbis say that the Holy One told Israel, 'My children, I have created everything in pairs—heaven and earth, sun and moon, Adam and Eve, this World and the World to Come; but I am One alone in the Universe.' (*Devarim Rabbah* ii, 22).

Belief in the absolute and indivisible Unity of God is an important principle of the Jewish Faith. He is perfect and complete in Himself. There is no other power besides Him or issuing from Him. God has no bodily form, and whenever He is described in terms that could apply to human beings, it is only to satisfy our limited intelligence.

The concept of One God has been voiced by Israel's great leaders from Moses onwards, and the declaration of His unity, as contained in the *Shema*, remains a dominant feature of our daily prayers. In the Morning and Evening Services we loudly proclaim our belief that God is One, and during our last moments on earth we recite the *Shema* as an expression of our confidence in His justice and mercy.

3 The Fatherhood of God

Is He not your Father who acquired you ? (Deut. xxxii, 6).

A close and personal bond exists between God and man. Having created the world, He watches over each individual with the loving care that a father gives his children and He sets the example they should follow. That is what is meant by the verse in Genesis '*God created man in His own image*' (i, 27). Every commandment given to the Children of Israel, through Moses, has this for its aim: that we model our lives on the example set by the Creator. We are to conduct our lives on the highest plane of ethical and social behaviour. *You shall be holy for I the Lord your God am Holy* (Lev. xix, 2). This relationship of Father and children is stressed very often in our prayers. Knowing we have a Father who takes a personal interest in all that we do gives us a sense of security and companionship, and spurs us to fulfil our tasks in life.

4 Man's Choice

I call heaven and earth to witness against you this day, that I have set before you life and death, the blessing and the curse, therefore choose life (Deut. xxx, 19).

By recognizing the close relationship between himself and God, and his duty to carry out His commandments, man co-operates with God in establishing a world based on holiness. This idea is expressed by the Rabbis when they show the man who walks in the ways of God as a partner to the Holy One in the work of creation (*Bereshith Rabbah* xliii, 9; *Shabbath* 10 a, etc.).

It might be supposed that since an all-knowing God can foresee everything that is about to happen, man has no free choice but must do as the Almighty determines. But the teaching of Judaism is that man is blessed with free will to do either good or evil and must bear the responsibility for his actions. He will be rewarded for his good deeds but will be punished if he conflicts with the will of his Creator.

5 God's Justice

Shall not the Judge of all the World do justly?
(Gen. xviii, 25).

Abraham's plea to God to save the city of Sodom lest the good be destroyed with the wicked is an illustration of our belief in God as a true and righteous Judge. He judges each man according to his deeds, by rewarding the righteous and punishing the wicked. But the Bible makes it clear that the purpose of punishment is to give man the chance to repent and start his life anew. *I have no pleasure in the death of the wicked, but that the wicked turn from his way and live* (Ezekiel xxxiii, 11). We shall see later, when dealing with the Day of Atonement, what a prominent place the idea of repentance occupies in Jewish thought. The quality of God's mercy with which His justice is associated consoles us in time of sorrow and distress when we accept His decision without question.

6 Revelation

You, yourselves, have seen that I have talked with you from heaven (Ex. xx, 19).

These words were spoken by God through Moses after the revelation at Mount Sinai, when the Ten Commandments were given to the people. Judaism teaches that God reveals His will through those whom He selects for special purposes. Noah received a personal communication after the flood, whereby a number of laws were to be obeyed by all men, whatever their creed. Abraham was taught by similar revelations how righteousness and justice should be established in the world. And to Moses was granted the highest degree of revelation—he was singled out to teach the Divine Laws and Commandments to the people of Israel, to establish a nation with holiness as its central ideal. The greatest prophet of all times, he combined leadership with humility.

Revelation reached its climax at Mount Sinai. The principles embodied in the Ten Commandments, the עֲשֶׂרֶת הַדִּבְּרוֹת (Ten Divine Utterances), have been acknowledged as the foundation of religious and moral conduct for all mankind. Israel was chosen for the mission of teaching the world the belief in One God and the brotherhood of all men.

Revelation did not end with the death of Moses but went on till the time of Malachi, the last of the prophets. The word prophet, as well as the Hebrew נָבִיא, means a speaker or preacher, moved by the spirit of God and called upon to be His messenger. The prophets were men with exceptional spiritual and intellectual powers, they were able to foresee events and warn people of disasters which would come to them if they kept on turning aside from God's teachings. These men, inspired with a passion for justice and truth, fearlessly proclaimed their message to king and subject alike. They demanded obedience to the Law revealed to Moses.

CHAPTER 2

THE TREE OF LIFE

It is a tree of life to those who lay hold of it (Proverbs
iii, 18).

This sentence, which we recite in our Synagogues when
the *Sepher Torah* is returned to the Ark, refers to the
blessings of wisdom. Our Rabbis identify wisdom with
the Torah, for every branch of knowledge stems from the
tree of the Torah revealed by God to Moses.

1 The Torah as our Inheritance

*Moses commanded us a law as an inheritance of the
congregation of Jacob* (Deut. xxxiii, 4).

The verse forms part of the final blessing of Moses
before he took leave of the people he had faithfully led for
forty years. Just as an inheritance is passed from father to
son, so the Torah was to be handed down from generation
to generation. The term Torah applies, in the first
instance, to the Written Law—תּוֹרָה שֶׁבִּכְתָב—found in the
Five Books of Moses. In its wider meaning it includes the
Oral Law—תּוֹרָה שֶׁבְּעַל פֶּה—which is essential for applying
the Written Law to everyday life.

Let us deal with the books of the Torah and the other
books of the Bible.

2 The Pentateuch

The Hebrew name for the Bible תַּנַ״ךְ is formed from the initials of its three sections תּוֹרָה, נְבִיאִים, כְּתוּבִים (The word 'Bible' comes from the Greek and means 'The Book'.) The Torah contains five books, familiarly known as the חֲמִשָׁה חוּמְשֵׁי תוֹרָה (the five 'fifth parts' of the Torah), or simply as the חוּמָשׁ. 'Pentateuch' is a Greek word meaning five books. The Hebrew names of the five books are taken from the first characteristic word of each book; whereas the titles in the English Bible, Genesis, Exodus, Leviticus, Numbers, Deuteronomy—all, except one, derived from the Greek—describe their main theme. Their contents are briefly as follows:

(i) בְּרֵאשִׁית *In the beginning* (*God created the heaven and the earth*).

The origin of the Universe and the beginnings of the human race are described and are followed by an account of Adam and Eve and their descendants. Man is taught how to lead a righteous life and serve God by a series of tests, illustrated by the experiences of Noah and the patriarchs Abraham, Isaac and Jacob. The last chapters deal with Joseph's rise to power, Jacob's settlement in Egypt and the deaths of both.

'Genesis' means: birth (of the world).

(ii) שְׁמוֹת (*These are*) *the names of* (*the Children of Israel who came into Egypt*).

The history of our ancestors reaches dramatic heights. The Israelites are freed from Egyptian slavery after Pharaoh's defiance and the Ten Plagues. Under the inspired leadership of Moses, guided by God, they reach Sinai and witness the Divine Revelation of the Ten Commandments. The first Sanctuary is erected, dedicated to the Service of God. Many laws are listed in this book, including laws about the Sabbath and the three Pilgrim Festivals, as well as the leading principles of civil law to safeguard the rights of the individual and his property.

'Exodus' means: departure (from Egypt).

(iii) וַיִּקְרָא *And (the Lord) called (unto Moses).*

The central theme is the ideal of holiness which should influence everyday action and thought. An account of the personal and congregational sacrifices is given. These are preceded by repentance and action, such as giving back property wrongfully taken from a neighbour. The sacred duties of the Levites and priests in the Sanctuary are described. Laws about purity and purification, Dietary Laws, and laws dealing with the Day of Atonement, the Festivals and marriage are given. Then there are the rules of man's conduct to his neighbour: love replacing hatred, the giving of a helping hand to a friend in need, and the care of the stranger, the poor and the friendless.

'Leviticus' means: the Levites.

(iv) בְּמִדְבַּר *(And the Lord spoke unto Moses) in the wilderness of (Sinai).*

The wanderings of the Israelites in the wilderness take up most of this book. The twelve spies' mission, Korah's rebellion, Balaam's forced blessing of Israel and Joshua's appointment as the future leader are described. And there is an account of the numbering of the people, the Priestly Blessing, and of the laws relating to the Red Heifer and *Tzitzith* (see p. 112).

The title 'Numbers' refers to the numbering of the people, which was twice carried out in the wilderness.

(v) דְּבָרִים *(These are the) words (which Moses spoke to all Israel).*

In three farewell addresses, Moses speaks to the new generation which grew up in the wilderness and reviews the events of forty years. He tells them the principal laws they should keep when they enter the Promised Land. The first and second paragraphs of the *Shema* (see p. 42) are given. The last chapter brings the life of Moses to an end—*And there has not arisen a prophet in Israel like unto Moses whom the Lord knew face to face.*

'Deuteronomy' means: the second Law.

3 The Prophets

In the second section of the Bible are two groups: (*a*) the earlier Prophets and (*b*) the later Prophets.

(*a*) The part dealing with the earlier Prophets, נְבִיאִים רִאשׁוֹנִים, is historical in character, but its underlying theme is the message, preached by all the prophets, that obedience to God by the king and by the nation brings security whereas disobedience brings disaster. The lives and teachings of the prophets Samuel, Nathan, Ahijah, Elijah and Elisha are presented.

The individual books in this group are:

(i) יְהוֹשֻׁעַ—JOSHUA: Canaan is conquered, after the crossing of the Jordan under Joshua's leadership, and the land is divided among the tribes. The mission of the two spies, the fall of Jericho, the sin of Achan and the battle at Gibeon, when 'the sun stood still,' are some of the incidents.

(ii) שׁוֹפְטִים—JUDGES: These were inspired leaders, who were chosen for their qualities of courage and patriotism to free the Israelites from their enemies. Among the chief characters are Deborah, Gideon, Jephthah and Samson.

(iii) שְׁמוּאֵל א׳ וּב׳—THE TWO BOOKS OF SAMUEL: The life of the prophet Samuel, the rise of the monarchy (with Saul becoming Israel's first King), and the succession and reign of David are described.

(iv) מְלָכִים א׳ וב׳—THE TWO BOOKS OF KINGS: Solomon succeeds David. After his death the country is divided into the kingdoms of Judah and Israel. The history of the Northern Kingdom begins with Jeroboam and ends with the conquest of Samaria in 722 B.C.E. by Sargon II, who had seized the Assyrian throne. Some of the better known figures of the period are Ahab, Elijah, Elisha and Jehu. The Southern Kingdom's history starts with Rehoboam and ends with the conquest of Jerusalem by Nebuchadnezzar, King of Babylon in 586 B.C.E. Among the famous personages are Hezekiah, Josiah and the Prophets Isaiah and Jeremiah.

(b) The section devoted to the later Prophets, נְבִיאִים אַחֲרוֹנִים, is sub-divided into two parts: the three 'major' prophets and the twelve 'minor' prophets. The difference between the two is: in the case of the major prophets many of their prophecies have been preserved and form larger books; but of the minor prophets' messages only a few have come down to us.

Isaiah, Jeremiah and Ezekiel are the three major prophets.

(i) יְשַׁעְיָהוּ—ISAIAH: He prophesied for some forty years from about 740 B.C.E., in the last year of Uzziah's reign, and during the reigns of Jotham, Ahaz and Hezekiah, Kings of Judah. Readily accepting the Divine call, Isaiah forcefully denounced religious hypocrisy, the decay of moral standards, oppression of the poor and dishonesty among princes and judges. He warned both rulers and people that defiance of God could only result in invasion by Assyria. Nevertheless, he foresaw the redemption of the Jewish people, restored through a righteous remnant, for the Children of Israel are God's witnesses to proclaim His truth among the nations. The day will come when Universal Peace will reign supreme and *nation shall not*

*lift up sword against nation, neither shall they learn war
any more.*

Many modern scholars say that the second part of the
Book of Isaiah (chapters xl to lxvi) was not written by the
author of the first part, and refer to the writer as Deutero,
i.e. the 'Second' Isaiah. One of their chief arguments is
that these chapters deal with the period of the exile in
Babylon, about 150 years after Hezekiah's death. But
those who keep to the traditional view of the unity of
authorship claim that it was well within the Prophet's
power to foresee the future exile and redemption from
captivity.

(ii) יִרְמְיָהוּ—JEREMIAH: He was born in Anathoth,
near Jerusalem, the son of a priest. He prophesied for
more than forty years, from the thirteenth year of King
Josiah's reign until after the Captivity in 586 B.C.E.; he
witnessed the tragic events which led to the destruction of
the Temple. Jeremiah, who received the Divine call at an
early age, set out, after the death of Josiah, to condemn
injustice and idol worship. He accused the false prophets
and priests of turning Temple worship into a mockery, and,
as a result, he was frequently imprisoned. But he went on
denouncing wrong-doing, his prophecies being preserved
by Baruch his scribe. Despite his sorrow at the turn of
events, Jeremiah was confident that, in time, the exiled
Jews would be restored to their own land and that *the
sound of joy and the sound of gladness* would be heard in
their cities.

(iii) יְחֶזְקֵאל—EZEKIEL: Also of priestly stock, Ezekiel
prophesied in Babylonia where he had been taken as
captive in 597 B.C.E. to share the exile of King Jehoiachin.
Through his influence, assemblies for prayer were
established and it was from these that the Synagogue
developed. Ezekiel stressed the individual responsibility

of each man for his actions. He encouraged the exiles by his messages of hope and comfort. His vision of the valley of dry bones, of which we read in Synagogue on *Shabbath Chol Hamoed* during *Pesach* showed his faith in the restoration of Israel, *I shall put my spirit in you and you shall live; and I shall place you upon your land.*

The twelve minor Prophets are known as the תְּרֵי עֲשַׂר—Aramaic for twelve. They are:

(i) הוֹשֵׁעַ—HOSEA: A contemporary of Isaiah, he denounced the evils he saw in the Northern Kingdom during the reign of Jeroboam II, in the middle of the eighth century B.C.E. Hosea shows the relationship of God and Israel as that of a husband and his unfaithful wife who would be forgiven if only she repented of her bad deeds. Then, says God, in the words of the prophet, *I will betroth you to Me forever; I will betroth you to Me in righteousness and in justice, in loving-kindness and in mercy. And I will betroth you to Me in faithfulness.*

(ii) יוֹאֵל—JOEL: We are not certain about the date of Joel's prophecy. Some say he was the earliest of the prophets, but others place him with Haggai and Zechariah, the prophets of the Return from Exile. Joel symbolizes the destruction of Judah by a plague of locusts. The nation will be destroyed unless the people repent—*Rend your hearts and not your garments*—he cries. His prophecy ends on a happy note of promised salvation.

(iii) עָמוֹס—AMOS: Amos was called by God from shepherding his flock. He fought against social injustice in Israel during the time of Jeroboam II. He warned the people that the oppression of the poor by the merciless rich could not be pardoned; neither could idol worship and immorality. God's chosen people, he said, would receive even heavier punishment than other nations if they did not change their ways. *Seek good and not evil, that you may live. And so the Lord, the God of hosts, will be with you.*

(iv) עֹבַדְיָה—OBADIAH: This book has only one chapter. It is a declaration against the people of Edom who cruelly delivered the fugitives escaping over the border to the enemy—evidently referring to Nebuchadnezzar's invasion in 586 B.C.E. *Though you exalt yourself as the eagle and set your nest amongst the stars, even then will I bring you down,* exclaims God through the mouth of the prophet.

(v) יוֹנָה—JONAH: The Book of Jonah, which is read at the *Minchah* service on *Yom Kippur* (see p. 85), shows how futile it is for man to try to escape his obligations towards God, and how true repentance can save a nation. Many commentators suggest that the prophet is to be identified with Jonah, the son of Amittai, who prophesied in the reign of Jeroboam II.

(vi) מִיכָה—MICAH: A younger contemporary of Isaiah, Micah condemns the corruption and tyranny of the nobles, judges and false prophets in the kingdom of Judah. True religion required by God is: *only to do justly and to love mercy and to walk humbly with your God.* Micah also tells of the Messianic age when universal peace will be established.

(vii) נַחוּם—NAHUM: By their savage treatment of those they conquered, the people of the Assyrian Empire typified all that was cruel and merciless, and Nahum foresaw their doom. He portrayed the terrible scene—caused by the coming onslaught on Nineveh, the Assyrian capital. No nation, he declared, could survive if it denied the Divine Law of humanity. Nineveh did, in fact, fall in the year 612 B.C.E., when it was besieged by the Medes who were in league with Babylonia.

(viii) חֲבַקּוּק—HABAKKUK: The question posed by Habakkuk (who was probably a contemporary of Jeremiah) is: why should a wicked nation like the Chaldeans be chosen to carry out God's punishment of Judah?—such a cruel nation will destroy the just together with the wicked. The reply he receives is that the pride of the Chaldeans will prove their downfall, but *the righteous shall live by his faith.*

(ix) צְפַנְיָה—ZEPHANIAH: Another contemporary of Jeremiah during Josiah's reign, this prophet warns evildoers that *the day of the Lord* is coming. Under God's final judgment the wicked will be destroyed and all who seek righteousness and humility will be saved.

(x) חַגַּי—HAGGAI: After the proclamation of Cyrus in the year 538 B.C.E. many Jews had returned to the Holy Land and the rebuilding of the Second Temple began. Haggai started his work among the people in 520 B.C.E., encouraging them to carry on the task which they had discontinued because of the Samaritans' hostility. *The glory of this latter house shall be greater than that of the former, saith the Lord of hosts.*

(xi) זְכַרְיָה—ZECHARIAH: A contemporary of Haggai, he, too, began to prophesy in 520 B.C.E. He stresses that righteous living is more important than material wealth: *Not by might nor by power, but by My spirit, saith the Lord of Hosts.* Jerusalem will become the centre of worship of the One God. *In that day shall the Lord be One, and His name One.*

(xii) מַלְאָכִי—MALACHI: The Second Temple had been completed in 516 B.C.E. but the people, indifferent to their religious duties, treated it with disrespect by offering blemished sacrifices. Malachi, who prophesied at about the time of Ezra, blamed the laxity of the priests and Levites who were not true to their sacred office. He preaches the message of the universal fatherhood of God and the brotherhood of man. *Have we not all one Father? Hath not one God created us?* He appeals to

25

Israel to obey the Torah. *Remember the law of Moses My servant.*

4 The Holy Writings: כְּתוּבִים

(i) תְּהִלִּים—PSALMS: Sung to music on a variety of occasions, the psalms offer thanks to God for His loving-kindness and mercy, plead for Divine forgiveness for wrong doing, and extol righteous conduct and speech. Of the one hundred and fifty psalms, seventy-three are stated to be composed by, or for, King David. Psalms were sung in the Temple by the Levites. For instance on *Succoth*, the fifteen *Shir Hamaaloth* (cxx-cxxxiv) were sung. A daily psalm was recited when the morning sacrifice was offered. Because of their universal application, many psalms are included not only in our *Siddur* (see p. 42) and *Machzor* (see p. 68) but also in the prayer books of other religions.

(ii) מִשְׁלֵי—PROVERBS: Much of Solomon's wisdom is to be found in this collection of sayings. Many of them praise knowledge and many are moral maxims for the conduct of everyday life. They stress the importance of wisdom, but *the fear of the Lord is the beginning of knowledge.* The last chapter describes the *Esheth Chayil*—the woman of worth: it is recited in Jewish homes by husbands on the Sabbath eve.

(iii) אִיּוֹב—JOB: Disaster comes to Job, and provides a background for discussing the problem of human suffering. In dramatic dialogues between Job and four of his friends, this theme is developed; and the conclusion reached is that man must have absolute Faith in all that God does. The book ends happily—Job's fortunes are restored.

The next five books are known as the חָמֵשׁ מְגִלּוֹת—the

26

five *Megilloth* or Scrolls. Each is read on an appropriate occasion in Synagogue.

(iv) שִׁיר הַשִּׁירִים—SONG OF SONGS: This love-song between a shepherd and his shepherdess (ascribed to King Solomon) was interpreted by our Rabbis as referring to the love of God for Israel at Sinai. It is read during *Pesach* (see p. 69).

(v) רוּת—RUTH: This is the story of the Moabitess who was an ancestress of David and who became a convert to Judaism. It tells of her encounter with Boaz during the harvest season. It is read on *Shavuoth* (see p. 72).

(vi) אֵיכָה—LAMENTATIONS: An elegy written, according to tradition, by Jeremiah on the destruction of the Temple. The Hebrew title comes from the first word in the book, *How* (lonely dwells the city that was full of people). Lamentations is read on the Ninth of *Av* (see p. 97).

(vii) קֹהֶלֶת—ECCLESIASTES (One who speaks to an Assembly): In search of the true aim of life, *Koheleth* discusses the value of pleasure, wealth and knowledge. In tone the book is generally pessimistic. It concludes that the highest virtue is to fulfil God's commandments, for *this is the whole duty of man*. The traditional view is that it was written by King Solomon. Ecclesiastes is read during the Festival of *Succoth* (see p. 76).

(viii) אֶסְתֵּר—ESTHER: The story of the heroism of Esther and Mordecai and the downfall of Haman is read on *Purim* (see p. 89).

(ix) דָּנִיֵּאל—DANIEL: The Book tells of the refusal of Daniel, during the Babylonian exile in the sixth century B.C.E., to eat forbidden food and worship idols. Loyalty to Jewish observance in the Diaspora is taught and the supremacy of God in the world is shown.

(x) עֶזְרָא—EZRA: This is an important book historically, beginning with the return of the Exiles from Babylon under Zerubbabel, by permission of King Cyrus, in 538 B.C.E. The Second Temple is rebuilt in spite of the Samaritans' opposition. Nearly eighty years later Ezra, the Scribe, leads a large number of exiles to Palestine from Babylonia. He introduces reforms, forbids inter-marriage and promotes the study of the Torah.

(xi) נְחֶמְיָה—NEHEMIAH: The cup-bearer of Artaxerxes, he obtains permission, in 444 B.C.E., to go to Jerusalem and is appointed Military Governor of Judea. He holds the post for twelve years. Nehemiah supervises the rebuilding of the destroyed walls and, with Ezra, ensures that the Jewish community shall adhere to the laws of the Torah.

(xii) דִּבְרֵי הַיָּמִים א׳ וב׳—THE TWO BOOKS OF CHRONICLES: This is a survey of Biblical history, which gives attention to the worship and priesthood of the Temple. It ends with the proclamation of Cyrus.

CHAPTER 3

FROM GENERATION TO GENERATION

1 The 613 Commandments

All the commandments which Jews are required to keep are based on the Torah. Some may seem less important than others, but we should remember the words of the *Pirke Avoth* (ii, 1): 'Be heedful of a light precept [one which does not need much effort and sacrifice] as of a grave one, for you do not know the grant of reward for each precept.' As we shall see, the laws about the Sabbath and Festivals, about food and about duties of man to his neighbour, are a few examples of commandments which are all part of the Divine Order. By keeping them we practise a life of holiness. The *Mitzvoth* must be observed if the Jew wishes to lead a happy, noble and righteous life. Moses made this clear when he said: *And now, O Israel, what does the Lord your God require of you, but to fear the Lord your God, to walk in His ways, and to love Him, and to serve the Lord your God with all your heart and with all your soul. To keep the commandments of the Lord and His statutes which I command you this day, for your good* (Deut. x, 12, 13).

According to an early tradition quoted by Rabbi Simlai in the Talmud, there were 613 commandments revealed to Moses, 248 of them positive ones and 365 prohibitions. A complete list of them is given by Maimonides in his introduction to the *Mishneh Torah*. They are known as the תַּרְיַ״ג מִצְוֹת—the numerical value of תַּרְיַ״ג being 613. Many of them, relating to the Temple and sacrifices, could not be observed after the Destruction. On the other hand, many apply to the everyday life of the Jew today, and it is with these we shall deal in this book.

2 The Oral Law

It is certain that the Written Law was supplemented by oral teaching and interpretation. If, for instance, we take the law against work on the Sabbath: only a few examples were given of what is meant by such work. The kindling of fire is specifically forbidden (Ex. xxxv, 3); walking beyond a certain limit is mentioned (Ex. xvi, 29) and gathering sticks (Num. xv, 32). From Ex. xvi, 23 and xxxiv, 21, we can see that cooking, baking, ploughing and harvesting are prohibited on the Sabbath. There must have been many acts of labour which were called 'work' and came under the Mosaic laws dealing with the Sabbath; and there must have been a large number of other precepts—relating to Festivals, *Kashruth*, Marriage and other matters.

So, along with the Written Law, was the Oral Law, and both derived their authority from the Divine revelation at Sinai. (Some evidence for the existence of the Oral Law is to be found elsewhere in the Bible, such as the references to the law against carrying burdens on the Sabbath, in Jeremiah xvii, 21f, and trading on the Sabbath, in Nehemiah x, 32; xiii, 15f.)

The first chapter of the *Pirke Avoth* tells us how the Oral Law was handed on from the time of Sinai: 'Moses received the Torah from Sinai and handed it down to Joshua; Joshua to the Elders, and the Elders to the Prophets; then the Prophets handed it down to the Men of the Great Synagogue.' It was then passed from generation to generation by the leading Rabbinic scholars who expounded the Oral Law until the time of R. Judah the Prince who arranged all the laws systematically in the Mishnah. And even after the Mishnah had been compiled, the Oral Law continued to be developed by religious authorities.

3 The Mishnah

The word מִשְׁנָה comes from the root *shanah*, 'to repeat,' so it means 'to learn' or 'teach' through repetition. It consists mainly of the oral teachings of the Rabbis who taught in the years 30 B.C.E. to 219 C.E., i.e. from the time of Hillel to Judah Hanasi, who were known as *Tannaim* (teachers). These teachings form the basis of what is called *Halachah* (the guiding and, therefore, authoritative principle of Law).

R. Judah Hanasi (135-219), a man with a brilliant mind, was a direct descendant of Hillel. He shouldered his high office of *Nasi*, or Prince of the Sanhedrin, with great dignity, and he undertook the preparation of the text of the Mishnah—which, next to the Bible, has been the main source of Jewish Law to the present day. Apart from *Halachah*, the Mishnah contains a number of ethical and moral teachings intended to uphold man's dignity and sanctity.

Though there are some scholars who are not certain whether the Mishnah was put in writing by R. Judah or whether it was passed on orally, there can be no doubt that if it had not been for his skilful labour many a tradition would have been lost to us.

4 The contents of the Mishnah

The Mishnah is divided into Six Orders: שִׁשָּׁה סְדָרִים, generally abbreviated to שַׁ׳ס. Each Order is divided into tractates, each tractate into chapters, and each chapter into paragraphs.

The Six Orders are as follows:

(i) סֵדֶר זְרָעִים—The Order relating to Seeds: this deals mainly with agricultural laws but the first Tractate *Berachoth* (Benedictions) includes such laws as those dealing with the *Shema*, the *Amidah*, the Grace after Meals and Blessings to be recited at various times.

(ii) סֵדֶר מוֹעֵד—The Order relating to Festivals.

(iii) סֵדֶר נָשִׁים—The Order relating to Women: the Order deals with the laws of marriage, vows, the Nazarite, etc.

(iv) סֵדֶר נְזִיקִין—The Order relating to Damages: various aspects of civil law such as damage to property, sales and the law of inheritance. Jewish Courts of Law and criminal procedure are also dealt with.

(v) סֵדֶר קָדָשִׁים—The Order relating to Holy Things: chiefly concerned with sacrifices. This Section includes the laws of *Shechitah* and dietary laws.

(vi) סֵדֶר טָהֲרוֹת—The Order relating to Purities: laws of ritual uncleanness; regulations dealing with the Red Heifer.

The first letters in the names of these Six Orders form the words זְמַן נָקֵט, by which they can be more easily remembered. The language of the Mishnah is, on the whole, pure Hebrew and developed naturally from the Hebrew of the Bible.

5 The Talmud

For almost 300 years after the Mishnah was compiled Rabbinical scholars went on expounding and developing the Oral Law. They are, therefore, known as *Amoraim* (interpreters). In their discussions, based on the Mishnah, they often engaged in long and difficult arguments to reach a true interpretation of a Biblical command. The subjects they dealt with include festivals and ceremonies, civil and criminal law, social conduct and education. Their commentary, written in Aramaic, is known as גְּמָרָא - completion, because it completes the Mishnah.

The text of the Talmud (Study) comprises the *Mishnah* together with the *Gemara*.

The Babylonian Talmud, known as the Talmud *Bavli*, contains nearly 3,000 pages which reflect the studies carried on at famous Babylonian Academies in Sura, Pumbeditha and elsewhere. The task of editing all this material was undertaken by Rav Ashi, head of the Sura Academy, in the early part of the fifth century. The final touches were given to it by Ravina ben Huna at the end of the fifth century. The influence of the *Bavli* has shaped the course of Jewish life up to the present day.

The Palestinian Talmud, known as the Talmud *Yerushalmi*, is about a seventh of the size of the *Bavli*. Roman oppression, especially when the Emperor Constantine adopted Christianity early in the fourth century, made the study of the Torah almost impossible in Palestine. The *Yerushalmi*—which, according to modern scholars, was finished about the beginning of the fifth century—has therefore come down to us in a form that is incomplete and not as lucid as the *Bavli*.

6 The Shulchan Arukh

After the Talmudic epoch, interpretation of Jewish Law was one of the chief occupations of the Geonim (Excellencies), who headed the Sura and Pumbeditha Academies, from the end of the sixth century to the beginning of the eleventh. They won renown for their knowledge and scholarship, and sent written replies to questions they received from all parts of the world. Many of these were preserved and they became known as Responsa or שְׁאֵלוֹת וּתְשׁוּבוֹת, questions and replies. Later Rabbinical authorities continued the practice, and many Responsa were published in book form. The need to collect the final decisions into one authoritative code was obvious, and a number of such collections were produced by the Geonim and other authorities. Outstanding among them are the *Mishneh Torah* and the *Shulchan Arukh*.

The מִשְׁנֵה תּוֹרָה—'The Second Law,' was compiled by Moses Maimonides (1135-1204), the famous Rabbi and philosopher, who spent most of his life in Cairo. Divided into fourteen books, it is a masterly work covering the whole field of Jewish Law. It is also known as the יָד הַחֲזָקָה ('Strong Hand')—the numerical value of the letters of the word יָד is fourteen.

The שֻׁלְחָן עָרוּךְ—The 'Table Arranged,' was completed by Joseph Caro (1488-1575) in Safed. It is divided into four parts:

(i) אֹרַח חַיִּים—The Path of Life: this deals with such everyday duties as Divine Worship, the Sabbath, Festivals and Fasts.

(ii) יוֹרֶה דֵעָה—Teacher of Knowledge: among the subjects are *Shechitah*, Dietary Laws, mourning; ethical duties including respect for parent and teacher; charity, the *Sepher Torah* and *Mezuzah*.

(iii) אֶבֶן הָעֵזֶר—Stone of Help: treating of all aspects of Marriage.

(iv) חֹשֶׁן מִשְׁפָּט—Breastplate of Judgment: on civil law.

This monumental work, together with the later annotations of Moses Isserles (1530-1572), a famous Polish Rabbi, has remained the standard authority for all Jewish Law and Practice.

CHAPTER 4

COMMUNAL WORSHIP
AND PRIVATE PRAYER

1 Prayer **2** The Synagogue and its Contents **3** The Synagogue Services **4** The Congregation **5** Private Prayer **6** The Blessings **7** The *Birkath Hamazon*

1 **Prayer**

The most natural way to come near to God is through prayer. There are moments in our lives when we crave to give thanks for blessings, when we seek consolation for sorrows, or when we want an answer to our needs and desires. To whom can we turn at such times but to our Father in Heaven? True prayer must come from the heart and be accompanied by devotion, expressed in Hebrew by the terms כַּוָּנָה or עִיּוּן תְּפִלָּה 'close attention to prayer.'

During prayers we must dedicate ourselves to the service of God and expel all other thoughts from the mind. It must not be a mechanical task, but a supplication for mercy and grace before the All-Present (*Avoth* ii, 18). God is always ready to hear sincere prayers. It may sometimes seem that they remain unanswered, but we must have complete confidence in God's justice and wisdom.

When Moses wanted God to heal Miriam of her leprosy, his prayer was simply: *O God, heal her now, I beseech Thee* (Num. xii, 13). Yet after the incident of the golden calf his prayer that the people be forgiven lasted forty days (Deut. ix, 25). In both cases the answer was

35

favourable. It is not the length of the prayer but its sincerity which is important.

2 The Synagogue and its Contents

The Tabernacle in the wilderness and the Temple in Jerusalem were, before the Exile, the main centres of public worship, and symbolized the presence of God among the people. Priests offered the daily sacrifices on behalf of the community and it was only on special occasions that the individual took part in the Service. During their exile in Babylon the Jews came together for prayer and study, and on their return under Zerubbabel, and later under Ezra, they continued this practice and the house of assembly became known as the בֵּית הַכְּנֶסֶת. The Synagogue—a Greek word also meaning house of assembly—developed side by side with the Second Temple, and its Services were arranged on the pattern of the sacrificial system.

In our Synagogues today are several features that remind us of the Tabernacle and Temple:

(i) The אֲרוֹן הַקֹּדֶשׁ—the *Holy Ark*, represents the Holy of Holies, the innermost part of the Sanctuary and Temple, where even the High Priest could enter only on the Day of Atonement (Lev. xvi). The Ark is built on the eastern wall so that when we pray we face the direction of the Temple's site in Jerusalem. In Israel the Jews living east of Jerusalem build the Ark in the western wall for a similar reason.

(ii) The נֵר תָּמִיד—the continual lamp hanging before the Ark represents the lamp which burnt continually in the Sanctuary (Ex. xxvii, 20).

(iii) The סֵפֶר תּוֹרָה containing the *Pentateuch* is deposited in the Ark. It must be written in square Hebrew characters by a סוֹפֵר, an expert and pious scribe, using black ink on specially prepared parchment. Over the breastplate hangs the יָד or pointer—it is used for the Reading of the Torah. The two rollers round which the scroll is wrapped are given the name of עֵץ חַיִּים—the tree of life—by which name the Torah is called (see p. 17). The gold and silver ornaments adorning the *Sepher Torah* remind us of the ornaments of the High Priest and are called כְּלֵי קֹדֶשׁ—sacred vessels.

(iv) The בִּימָה or *Almemar* (the word is Arabic and means 'platform') was at one time used only for the Reading of the Law and *Haphtarah*, and for Rabbinical discourses. In some Synagogues the Reader—known as the חַזָּן or שְׁלִיחַ צִבּוּר (representative of the Congregation) —leads the Congregation in prayer from a place lower than the Ark. This custom is based on the verse *Out of the depths have I called to You, O Lord* (Ps. cxxx, 1).

(v) In obedience to the law contained in the Second Commandment, 'You shall not make unto yourself any graven image nor any likeness . . .' No Images or statues are permitted in the Synagogue.

(vi) *Instrumental Music* was forbidden in Synagogues on Sabbaths and Holy-days by the Rabbis; only in the Temple was music permitted on these days when sacrifices were offered. So the absence of music reminds us of the destruction of the Temple.

(vii) *Women* are separated from men, just as in Temple times. The intention is: maintaining propriety and decorum during the Service.

The association of the Synagogue with education began in very early days. The elementary school was for a long time next door to the Synagogue and so was the *Beth Hamidrash*, the school for higher learning. In time the Synagogue became the meeting-place for students and scholars. Many Synagogues today have a small room attached to them, known as a *Beth Hamidrash*, where regular courses in Rabbinic studies are conducted, especially on Sabbaths.

3 The Synagogue Services

The custom of praying three times daily is to be found in the Bible. We read, for instance, that Daniel *got down upon his knees three times a day and prayed and gave thanks before his God, as he had done previously* (Dan. vi, 11). After the Second Temple had been destroyed and the sacrifices had stopped, prayer became the binding and unifying force among the Jews. Fixed periods for daily prayer, introduced by the Rabbis, corresponded with the times when the sacrifices had been offered. The שַׁחֲרִית—Morning prayer—and מִנְחָה—Afternoon prayer—correspond with the daily morning and afternoon sacrifices. The מַעֲרִיב—Evening prayer—corresponds with the nightly burning of fats and limbs. There was no public sacrifice in the evening, and the reciting of the evening *Amidah* was considered by some Rabbis as optional. The custom to recite it gradually became obligatory, as it is nowadays; but to meet this other view the evening *Amidah* is not repeated aloud by the *Chazzan* and there is no *Kedushah*.

On Sabbaths, *Rosh Chodesh*, and Festivals there is the מוּסָף—additional service, corresponding with the additional offering sacrificed in the Temple on these days.

4 The Congregation

When Jews assemble for תְּפִלָּה בְּצִבּוּר, congregational prayer, at least ten males over the age of thirteen must be present: they are known as a מִנְיָן, i.e. (requisite) number. The Synagogue, as a spiritual centre, unites Jews all over the world; it creates an atmosphere of devotion and religious feeling. Praying together with our fellow-man makes us conscious that we are all members of one great community and inspires us with loyalty to our religion. It reminds us that Hebrew is the language of the Bible, of our prayers, and of our people. It has proved important, through the ages, in preserving Judaism and the Jewish nation.

5 **Private Prayer:** תְּפִלַּת יָחִיד

Some of the prayers now recited in the Synagogue were originally said in the home. These include practically all the prayers in the first part of the Morning Service and others composed by Rabbis probably for their own use. Two examples are the concluding prayer of the *Amidah*, 'O my God, guard my tongue from evil,' which was written by Mar, son of Ravina, and the *Yehi Ratzon*—recited on the Sabbath before *Rosh Chodesh*—by Rav.

Synagogue worship need not exclude private prayer offered spontaneously when we wish to pour out our hearts to God. There are several such prayers in the Bible—uttered by the Patriarchs, by Moses and by the Prophets, among others. Not all of us are able to express ourselves adequately and we find in the Prayer Book a number of individual prayers to be recited on certain occasions, such as the prayer before retiring to rest at night and supplications by the sick and by travellers going on a long journey.

When we cannot attend the daily services at the Synagogue, we should say our prayers at home. The following, which are recited only when a *Minyan* is present, are then omitted: the *Kaddish*, *Borechu*, the repetition of the *Amidah*, the *Kedushah*, the Priestly Blessing and the Reading of the Law.

6 The Blessings: בְּרָכוֹת

It would be unworthy of us to enjoy God's protection and bounty without expressing our thanks to Him. No man, our Rabbis say, should enjoy anything in this world unless he has previously uttered a blessing. Most blessings are of ancient origin and usually begin with the words 'Blessed art Thou O Lord our God, King of the Universe.' Even on sad occasions a blessing has to be recited acknowledging the justice of God. In this way we show our complete faith in His will.

Maimonides, in his *Mishneh Torah*, divides the Benedictions into three groups: (*a*) Blessings that express our thanks to God for the things we enjoy, such as the blessings said over bread, fruit, etc. (*b*) Blessings which praise Him for granting us the privilege of carrying out a religious duty, such as the *Mezuzah*, *Tzitzith*, etc. (*c*) Blessings of thanksgiving and praise, such as those in the early part of the Morning Service and in the *Amidah*.

7 The Grace after Meals: בִּרְכַּת הַמָּזוֹן

And you shall eat and be satisfied and bless the Lord your God for the good land which He has given you (Deut. viii, 10).

This verse, say our Rabbis, imposes on us the duty to say a blessing after a meal. Originally, the Grace after Meals consisted of three paragraphs in which (*a*) we thank God for giving us sustenance; (*b*) we thank Him for letting us inherit the land of Israel and the Torah; and (*c*) we pray that Jerusalem shall be rebuilt and the Temple Service restored. Later a fourth paragraph was added, containing the words 'Who is good and does good.' After the fall, in 135 C.E., of Bethar, where Bar Cochba made his last stand, the Emperor Hadrian refused for some time to allow the dead to be buried. When, at long last, permission was granted, this blessing was composed.

The short prayers at the end of the Grace after Meals, all beginning with הָרַחֲמָן — 'the All-Merciful' — were added still later. On Sabbaths and Festivals prayers are offered which specially apply to the occasion. When three or more males over the age of thirteen have their meal together the Grace is introduced by what is known as a זִמּוּן — 'an invitation' to prayer — one of them takes the lead in calling on the others to offer thanks; the company is known as a *Mezumman*. The introduction used on this occasion varies slightly when there are ten or more present, or at festivities such as a wedding banquet.

CHAPTER 5

SOME OUTSTANDING FEATURES OF THE SYNAGOGUE SERVICE

1 The Siddur

Prayers, as we saw in the last chapter, formed part of the Temple Service. We know from the Talmud that psalms were sung by the Levites, especially on festivals, and the daily prayers in the Temple included the *Shema* with its accompanying blessings, the Ten Commandments and the Priestly Blessing. The Men of the Great Synagogue (fifth century B.C.E.), according to tradition, instituted a number of prayers including the *Kiddush*, *Havdalah* and *Amidah*, and others were composed in later centuries; so by the time the Talmud was finally edited in the sixth century the essentials of the Synagogue Service we know today had been established. The first authority to compile a complete סִדּוּר (i.e. arrangement or order of Service), was Rav Amram, the Gaon of Sura, who died about the year 875.

The two main foundations of the Service are the *Shema* and the *Amidah*.

2 The Shema

You shall speak of them when you lie down and when you rise up (Deut. vi, 7). In accordance with this command we recite the *Shema* during the Morning and Evening Services. It consists of the following three paragraphs:

42

(i) Deut. vi, 4-9, beginning with שְׁמַע יִשְׂרָאֵל—*Hear, O Israel* (*the Lord our God, the Lord is One*). This verse, which teaches the Unity of God, has become known as the Jewish Declaration of Faith. The paragraph reminds us of our duty to love God with all our heart, to meditate constantly over His commandments and to impress them upon our children. It also contains the laws of the *Tephillin* and *Mezuzah*.

(ii) Deut. xi, 13-21, beginning with וְהָיָה אִם שָׁמֹעַ תִּשְׁמְעוּ —*and if you will hearken diligently*. Besides repeating many of the sentences of the first paragraph this section deals with the lesson of reward and punishment, illustrated by the blessing of rain so essential to the farmer in Palestine. Obedience to God's Will, it teaches, brings happiness, whereas disobedience results only in sorrow.

(iii) Num. xv, 37-41, beginning with וַיֹּאמֶר ה׳—*And the Lord said*. This part contains the command relating to the צִיצִית, *that you may look on it and remember all the commandments of the Lord and do them*.

3 The Shemoneh Esreh

The שְׁמוֹנֶה עֶשְׂרֵה—the eighteen Benedictions—were not all composed at the same time. They were written at various periods between the time of the Men of the Great Assembly and the end of the first century C.E., and received their final form under Rabban Gamliel II of Javneh, the head of Palestine Jewry c. 80-117. There are, actually, nineteen prayers: the additional one, according to some scholars, was the prayer beginning with the word וְלַמַּלְשִׁינִים—'for the slanderers let there be no hope.' It was composed by Samuel the Younger at the request of Rabban Gamliel, to condemn those Jewish slanderers who rejected the Torah and denounced their brethren to the authorities. Others believe that there were only

43

seventeen paragraphs before the prayer against the slanderers was added; and they account for the present division of nineteen by referring to the view, expressed in the Talmud, that the two blessings (xiv and xv) 'for the rebuilding of Jerusalem' and 'for the restoration of the dynasty of David' were originally combined but later separated.

Other names for the *Shemoneh Esreh* are the עֲמִידָה—the prayer recited whilst standing—and the תְּפִלָּה—THE prayer.

The first three and last three benedictions of the *Amidah* are recited at every Service; the thirteen intermediary prayers, recited only on weekdays, are replaced on Sabbaths and Festivals by one prayer dealing with aspects of the Holy Day.

In the first group are three Blessings of Praise to God, in the second national and personal Petitions, and in the third Blessings of Thanksgiving.

The nineteen prayers are these:

(i) Expressing praise to God, who remembers the pious deeds of the patriarchs on our behalf;

(ii) Declaring God's might in sustaining the living and His Power to revive the dead;

(iii) Praising the Holiness of God;

(iv) Asking for understanding and knowledge;

(v) For assisting our efforts to return to God in perfect repentance;

(vi) For forgiveness for any sins we may have committed;

(vii) For deliverance from affliction and persecution;

(viii) For bodily health;

(ix) Asking God to bless the produce of our fields so that we may be free from want;

(x) For the ingathering of the exiles;

   (xi) For the rule of Justice under righteous leaders;

  (xii) For protection against slanderers who denounce their fellow-men;

 (xiii) For the reward of the righteous and pious;

 (xiv) For the rebuilding of Jerusalem, and

  (xv) For the restoration of the dynasty of David;

 (xvi) Asking God to accept our prayers in mercy and favour;

(xvii) For the restoration of the Divine Service in the Temple;

(xviii) Thanksgiving for God's mercies;

 (xix) For the granting to Israel of the blessing of peace.

A number of prayers which are added on special occasions are set out in the Daily Prayer Book.

In the Synagogue, during the repetition of the *Amidah*, the קְדוּשָׁה—sanctification, recited after the second Blessing, consists of scriptural verses in which the Holiness, Glory and Eternal Sovereignty of God are proclaimed.

4 The Shacharith Service

The main elements of the daily Morning Service are:

  (i) בִּרְכוֹת הַשַּׁחַר—'Blessings relating to the Dawn.' These include some benedictions expressing gratitude to God for His care and protection by granting our personal needs.

 (ii) פְּסוּקֵי דְזִמְרָא—Verses of Song, consisting mainly of selections from the Psalms. This section begins with בָּרוּךְ שֶׁאָמַר and ends with יִשְׁתַּבַּח.

(iii) The *Shema*, with its accompanying blessings.

(iv) The *Amidah*.

 (v) תַּחֲנוּן—After the *Amidah*, 'prayers of supplication,' in which we ask God to pardon our sins, are recited. On

Mondays and Thursdays these prayers are increased, but on festive and some other occasions they are left out.

(vi) The Reading of the Law on Mondays and Thursdays. This is dealt with in Section 6 of this Chapter.

(vii) עָלֵינוּ לְשַׁבֵּחַ —'It is our duty to praise.' The *Alenu*, a prayer which concludes all Divine Services, has two parts: the first proclaims God as King of Israel; the second looks forward to the time when idolatry will disappear, when all mankind will acknowledge God as King of the Universe, and *in that day shall the Lord be One and His name One.*

Originally, *Alenu* was part of the *Musaph* Service recited on *Rosh Hashanah* where it introduced the Biblical texts on God's Sovereignty (see p. 81). Because of the sublime nature of its message, the prayer was eventually recited at the end of every Service.

5 The Kaddish

The קַדִּישׁ —sanctification—is an Aramaic prayer that takes various forms in the *Siddur*. It expresses the hope for universal peace under the Kingdom of God, and was recited originally at the end of a reading from the Bible or a Halachic discourse. The prayer was composed in Aramaic because that language was spoken and understood by Jews after the Babylonian exile. The response 'May His Great Name be blessed' is of ancient origin: it was recited, in Hebrew, in the days of the Temple. Gradually, the *Kaddish* prayer was introduced into the Synagogue Prayers to mark the completion of the principal sections of the Service as follows:—

(i) חֲצִי קַדִּישׁ —half *Kaddish* said at the end of a section of the Service, and

(ii) קַדִּישׁ שָׁלֵם —complete *Kaddish*—said at the end of

the Service. It is also known as the קַדִּישׁ תִּתְקַבַּל from the first word of the additional sentences.

Other forms of the *Kaddish* include (a) קַדִּישׁ אֲבֵלִים or קַדִּישׁ יָתוֹם (the Mourners' *Kaddish*). This is recited by an orphan for eleven months after the death of a parent, and on the anniversary of a parent's death. Reverence for parents continues after their death; and through the sanctification of God's name and submission to His Will, the child continues in the tradition of his parents and thereby shows them respect and honour; and (b) קַדִּישׁ דְּרַבָּנָן—The *Kaddish* recited after the study of Rabbinical writings or a Rabbinical discourse. One of its passages asks for a blessing on all engaged in teaching and studying the Torah.

6 The Reading of the Law: קְרִיאַת הַתּוֹרָה

Public readings from the Torah began in early times. The Bible refers to some of them. Moses commanded the priests and Levites to read the Law, after each seven-year cycle, to the people assembled on *Succoth*, that *they may hear and learn and fear the Lord your God and observe to do all the words of this Law* (Deut. xxxi, 12). The Talmud says that Moses taught the people to read from the Torah on Sabbaths, Festivals, *Chol Hamoed* and *Rosh Chodesh*. Ezra, the scribe, and the Levites read the Law to the people and *gave the sense and caused them to understand the reading* (Nehemiah viii, 8). In addition, readings were given on Monday and Thursday mornings. These were market days when the Courts of Law were in session and there was sure to be a large audience.

Regular readings of the Law on Sabbaths and Festivals probably developed from the strong opposition of Jewish leaders and Rabbis to the views of the Samaritans and the Sadducees, who accepted only the written Law and denied the Oral Law's validity. At first, suitable passages would be read before Festivals, starting perhaps with the four special Sabbaths, when Rabbis would interpret the laws which the people should follow in accordance with tradition. The practice gradually spread to every Sabbath and Festival, and was well established before the first century. A difference of custom between the Jews of Babylon and those of Palestine was: the former read through the Torah once a year, whereas the latter read it once every three years—hence the term 'Triennial Cycle.'

The Pentateuch is divided into fifty-four sections, each one known as a סִדְרָא—'Order' or 'Section.' Each *Sidra* is sub-divided into portions each of which is called a פָּרְשָׁה. Before the Reading of the Law, the Ark in the Synagogue is opened—פְּתִיחָה—and the scrolls, *Siphre Torah* are 'taken out'—הוֹצָאָה. The number of males 'called up' to the Reading varies: on Sabbath, seven; on *Yom Kippur*, six; on *Rosh Hashanah* and the Pilgrim Festivals, five; on *Rosh Chodesh* and *Chol Hamoed*, four; on *Purim*, *Chanucah* and fast days, three; and on Sabbath afternoons and Monday and Thursday mornings (when the first *Parashah* of the forthcoming weekly *Sidra* is read), three. The 'calling-up' is known as an עֲלִיָה—'going up' (to the *Bimah*).

At one time every person called up read his own portion, but afterwards, in order that the unlearned should not be put to shame, a בַּעַל קְרִיאָה—expert in Reading the Law—was appointed to intone the whole *Sidra*. The first three people to be called up are a *Cohen*, a *Levi* and a *Yisrael*—to give each of the divisions in Jewry, as it were, the honour of taking part in the ceremony.

After the Reading of the Law, the *Sepher Torah* is

'lifted up' for all to see—הַגְבָּהָה. Then it is 'rolled together'—גְּלִילָה—its mantle and ornaments are replaced, and it is 're-entered' in the Ark—הַכְנָסָה.

7 Haphtarah: הַפְטָרָה

This word means 'conclusion', i.e. concluding the Reading of the Torah with a passage from the Prophets. The person who is called up for the conclusion of the Reading from the Law reads the *Haphtarah* and is referred to as the מַפְטִיר. The particular selection from the Prophets contains a message corresponding with the *Sidra* of the day.

It is generally supposed that the reading of the *Haphtarah* started in this way: during periods of persecution, such as that of Antiochus of Syria (168-165 B.C.E.), study of the Torah was forbidden, and, instead, the Jews read a passage from the Prophets which had some relation to the *Sidra*; for this would escape the notice of the persecutors since, unlike the Torah, the *Haphtarah* did not have to be read from a specially prepared scroll of parchment. It is preferable, however, to assume that the *Haphtarah* was introduced by the Rabbis to show that religious leaders and Prophets, who came after Moses, also subscribed to the Oral Law. As with the Reading of the Law, it was instituted to refute the views of the Sadducees.

At first the *Haphtarah* would be read only on Festivals —on *Pesach*, for instance, when the accounts of Joshua's and Josiah's celebration of the Festival would form the basis of the Rabbi's address when he interpreted the Oral Law. With time the custom spread until the *Haphtarah* was read during the Morning Services of Sabbath, Festivals, and Fast-days, and at *Minchah* on *Yom Kippur*.

8 **Hallel:** הַלֵּל

The group of psalms cxiii to cxviii is known as *Hallel* (Praise). In Talmudic times this group was known as the 'Egyptian' *Hallel*, because the second psalm (cxiv) begins with the words *When Israel went forth out of Egypt*. This was to distinguish it from another psalm (cxxxvi), called the 'Great' *Hallel*, which is recited on Sabbaths and Festivals during the Morning Service. Each verse ends with the refrain *For His loving-kindness endures forever*.

The complete *Hallel* is said on the first two days of *Pesach*, on both days of *Shavuoth*, on the nine days of *Succoth* and the eight days of *Chanucah*. חֲצִי הַלֵּל—'half,' or rather part of, *Hallel*—is said on the intermediate days (*Chol Hamoed*) and last two days of *Pesach*, when two sections are omitted. One reason for this, given by our Rabbis, has to do with the crossing of the Red Sea which occurred on the 7th day of the Festival. The ministering Angels desired to sing a song to God while the Egyptians were drowning, but God said 'Shall you sing praises to me whilst my children are sinking in the sea?' On *Rosh Chodesh* (New Moon) the two paragraphs are omitted because it is a minor festival.

Hallel is not recited on *Rosh Hashanah* or *Yom Kippur* because—say the Rabbis—God is then sitting on His Throne of Judgment, and it would not be fitting for Israel to sing a joyous song on so solemn an occasion. Neither is *Hallel* recited on *Purim* (the Feast of Lots), because no praise is sung to God for miracles which occurred outside *Eretz Yisrael*. Furthermore, the reading of the *Purim* story (the *Megillah*) in itself constitutes a *Hallel* or praise to God.

CHAPTER 6

FROM NEW MOON TO NEW MOON

1 The Jewish Calendar **2** *Rosh Chodesh* **3** *Yomtov Sheni*
4 Some Interesting Formulæ

1 **The Jewish Calendar**

The Jewish Calendar reckons the duration of each month according to the time the moon takes to complete one revolution round the earth, i.e. about 29½ days. The twelve Jewish months accordingly consist of either 29 or 30 days, making a total of 354 days a year. The lunar year is thus 11 days less than the solar year of 365 days—the time it takes the earth to make one revolution round the sun. To ensure that the Festivals are celebrated in their proper seasons—e.g. Passover in spring, and Tabernacles in autumn—an additional month, *Adar Rishon*, has to be inserted in the Calendar seven times in 19 years, adjusting the lunar year to the solar year. These leap years occur in the 3rd, 6th, 8th, 11th, 14th, 17th and 19th year of each nineteen-year cycle.

The day of the Jewish Calendar lasts from sunset to sunset—*And it was evening and morning, one day* (Gen. i, 5) —and there are seven days in the week.

2 **The New Moon:** רֹאשׁ חֹדֶשׁ

The permanent calendar was fixed by Hillel II, a direct descendant of the famous Hillel, together with a number of Rabbinical scholars, about the year 359 C.E. In the preceding centuries the New Moon and, therefore, the first day of the month, could be determined only by

careful observation of the sky. This was of great importance for ensuring that the Festival occurring in any
particular month should be observed at its proper time.
As the *Mishnah Rosh Hashanah* explains, the New month
was proclaimed as *Mekuddash* (sanctified), on the evidence
of witnesses claiming to have seen the New Moon, who
were thoroughly examined by the Sanhedrin, the highest
Court in Israel. The examination took place on the 30th
day of the month. If the witnesses' testimony was
accepted, that day was proclaimed *Rosh Chodesh*, and the
previous month had only 29 days. If their testimony was
not accepted, or if no witnesses came forward, the following day was proclaimed *Rosh Chodesh*, and the preceding
month had 30 days.

3 Yomtov Sheni

Now, the Jewish communities outside Palestine, mainly
centred in Babylon, could never be reached in a day by
the messengers of the Jerusalem Sanhedrin, who were
sent out to inform them of its decision. Indeed it sometimes took as much as fourteen or fifteen days to reach
them, and they would be wondering whether *Rosh
Chodesh* had been proclaimed by the Sanhedrin after the
29th or 30th day of the previous month, as explained
above. So, to make sure they were observing the month's
Festival on the right day, Jewish communities outside
Israel kept two holy days when only one was
prescribed by the Torah—i.e. the 1st and 7th days of
Passover, the one day of Pentecost, and the 1st and 8th day
of Tabernacles. The exception was *Yom Kippur*, for it was
felt that fasting on two days would be too great a hardship.
Rosh Hashanah was, and still is, observed even in the Holy
Land on two days, as there was always some uncertainty
whether the Sanhedrin would fix the first of *Tishri* (when

Rosh Hashanah falls) on the 30th of *Elul* or on the following day.

Even after the Calendar was fixed, and up to the present day, the יוֹם טוֹב שֵׁנִי שֶׁל גָּלֻיּוֹת—the second day of the Festival in the Diaspora—continued to be observed outside Palestine.

4 Some Interesting Formulae

The *Shulchan Arukh* (*Orach Chayyim* 428, para. 1) gives some helpful numerical combinations relating to the Calendar. Here are two of them:

(i) לֹא אַדַ״וּ רֹאשׁ—i.e. the first day of *Rosh Hashanah* cannot fall on a Sunday, Wednesday or Friday.

If *Rosh Hashanah* fell on a Sunday, then *Hoshana Rabba* (*Tishri* 21st) would occur on the Sabbath, when it would be forbidden to shake the *Lulav* and beat the willows. If it fell on a Wednesday or Friday *Yom Kippur* would occur on a Friday or Sunday respectively, the day before or after the Sabbath; and this would create great difficulties.

(ii) לֹא בַּדַ״וּ פֶּסַח—i.e. the first day of *Pesach* cannot fall on a Monday, Wednesday or Friday. If it did, *Hoshana Rabba* and *Yom Kippur* would again fall on or near the Sabbath respectively.

CHAPTER 7

THE DAY OF DELIGHT

1 The Sabbath Day

Remember the Sabbath day to keep it holy. Six days you shall labour, and do all your work; but the seventh day is a sabbath unto the Lord your God: in it you shall not do any work, you, or your son, or your daughter, your manservant, or your maidservant, or your cattle, or your stranger who is within your gates: for in six days the Lord made heaven and earth, the sea and all that is therein, and rested on the seventh day: wherefore the Lord blessed the Sabbath day and hallowed it (Ex. xx, 8ff).

The Fourth Commandment tells us that by observing the Sabbath's holiness we re-affirm our belief in God who created the world for the benefit of mankind. One day a week is to be set aside, not merely to rest from our weekly toil, but to keep it holy by spiritual endeavour: it is a day for refreshing both body and soul.

There is another aspect of the Sabbath day. In the version of the Fourth Commandment to be found in Deuteronomy v, 15, no reference is made to the Creation. We read instead: *and you shall remember that you were a slave in the land of Egypt and the Lord your God brought you out from there with a mighty hand and an outstretched arm; therefore the Lord your God commanded you to keep the Sabbath day.* The Sabbath thus also reminds us of

54

God as our Redeemer and becomes a symbol of Israel's permanent freedom from bondage. It is an 'everlasting covenant' and a 'sign between God and the Children of Israel for ever' (Ex. xxxi, 16 and 17).

Let us deal with some of the chief observances by which we sanctify the Sabbath.

2 A Day of Holiness

Kiddush—קִדּוּשׁ. The prayer of the 'sanctification of the Day,' as the Rabbis call it, is recited in Synagogue on Sabbath Eve, towards the end of the *Maariv* Service, and at home before we partake of the evening meal. It consists of two blessings. The first is over wine—we are told by the Rabbis to remember the Sabbath Day over wine, which is a symbol of joy 'gladdening the heart of man' (Ps. civ, 15). The second blessing points to the day's twofold character that we have just discussed: it is a 'memorial of the Creation' and the first of the holy assemblies for worship on holy days mentioned in Lev. xxiii, in 'remembrance of the departure from Egypt.'

Originally *Kiddush* was recited in the Synagogue so that visitors, or the poor who lodged in the Synagogue on Friday night, could take part in the ceremony before sitting down to their evening meal. Though circumstances changed, the custom remained, and *Kiddush* is heard in Synagogue every Friday and Festival evening except the first two nights of Passover when even the poorest must be provided with four cups of wine at the *Seder* Service in someone's home. Another form of *Kiddush* is recited at home on Sabbath morning before we start our meal.

At the three Sabbath Services in Synagogue, devotion to our Prayers can well prove a sanctifying influence on our minds and hearts. The 'reception of the Sabbath' on Friday night is known as קַבָּלַת שַׁבָּת. As early as Talmudic

times the Sabbath was hailed as a bride for whom Israel
waits eagerly after six days' absence. Following a custom
which originated in Safed in the sixteenth century, we
receive the Sabbath by reciting six psalms (xcv to xcix
and xxix), commencing with לְכוּ נְרַנְּנָה. In addition, the
לְכָה דוֹדִי—'come my friend' (to meet the bride)—is
chanted. This poem was composed in the sixteenth century by Shelomoh Halevi (called Alkabetz) of Safed in
the form of an acrostic on the letters of his name. An
essential part of the morning service (*Shacharith*) is the
reading of the weekly *Sidra* from the Torah followed
by the *Haphtarah*. At the afternoon service (*Minchah*),
the first *parashah* of the coming week's *Sidra* is read.

During the long days of summer, from the Sabbath
after *Pesach* to the Sabbath before *Rosh Hashanah*, part
of the *Minchah* service on Sabbaths is devoted to the
reading of the Ethics of the Fathers, a custom which was
followed already in the Gaonic period. The sayings and
moral teachings of these 'Ethics' have ever remained a
valuable guide to right living. On the other Sabbaths
Psalm civ and the group of fifteen psalms (cxx-cxxxiv)
known as 'The Songs of Degrees'—שִׁיר הַמַּעֲלוֹת—are
recited. Hebrew and kindred studies are pursued on
Sabbaths, giving intellectual pleasure.

Havdalah—הַבְדָּלָה. Just as the *Kiddush* ushers in the
Sabbath, so does the *Havdalah*—'division' or 'separation'
of Sabbath from weekdays—say farewell to the day of rest.
There are four blessings. The first is over wine. The
second is over spices—recalling an early custom when, at
the end of a meal, spices were brought into the room on
burning coals to spread a sweet odour. In addition, the
perfume provides comfort to the departing 'additional
soul'—נְשָׁמָה יְתֵרָה—with which man is endowed on the
Sabbath day, according to our poetic Rabbis. By this they

imply that on Sabbath the soul's power is increased while the body's weariness is lessened. The third blessing is over light, the kindling of which indicates the close of the Sabbath and reminds us that light was created on the first day. The *Havdalah* candle is made of several twisted strands, since the blessing ends: 'Creator of the *lights* of the fire.' The fourth blessing concludes with praise of God who 'makes a distinction' between holy and profane.

3 A Day to Honour

In accordance with the Fourth Commandment we honour the Sabbath by refraining from weekday work. The religious implications of this were mentioned in paragraph 1, but the stoppage of work has also a social significance. After six days' toil the tired body needs rest, and this should be enjoyed not only by members of the household but by the servants and even by the cattle—an illustration of the Jewish feeling about the treatment of animals.

Only a few instances are given in the Torah of acts that would constitute labour on the Sabbath. Our Rabbis deduce that there are thirty-nine principal kinds of work—ל״ט מְלָאכוֹת—from the passages dealing with the building of the Tabernacle. Among them is inserted the command to rest on the Sabbath (Ex. xxxv, 2). They include ploughing, sowing, reaping, threshing, sewing, writing, kindling fire, carrying.

In addition, a number of acts are prohibited because they would lead to a desecration of the Sabbath. The terms for these are שְׁבוּת and גְּזֵרָה—acts prohibited on Sabbath and Festivals as decreed by our Rabbis. A further Rabbinical prohibition is classed as מוּקְצֶה—'set aside' or excluded from our mind. In effect, it forbids the handling on Sabbath of objects not intended for Sabbath use such as money, or lamps. The only time a Sabbath law may be broken is when life is in danger: the saving of life overrides any other consideration.

It is impossible to give more than a few ideas of the sort of work prohibited on Sabbath. The complete laws, given in the *Shulchan Arukh*, require careful study.

4 A Day of Delight

The description of Sabbath, in Isaiah lviii, 13, as a day of delight indicates the frame of mind in which we should approach the holy day. Far from being a day of gloom, it should spread joy and happiness. In the home on the eve of Sabbath the Friday night table, symbolic of the Altar of old, is adorned with candles, loaves and wine. The kindling of the lights by the mother of the household heralds the start of a day of light and cheer. Two candles at least, are lit, reminding us of the two forms of the first word of the Fourth Commandment—זְכוֹר—'remember' (Ex. xx, 8) and שָׁמוֹר—'observe' (Deut. v, 12).

The two loaves (*Challoth*) remind us of the double portion of manna—hence the term לֶחֶם מִשְׁנֶה—which, on Friday, was provided for the Israelites in the wilderness to last them two days; for they were forbidden to gather it on the Sabbath. The cloth beneath the loaves and the cover above them represent the dew which enwrapped the manna.

A beautiful Friday evening custom is the father's blessing of his children on their return from Synagogue while he recites the prayer offered by Jacob when blessing Ephraim and Manasseh. The mother, too, receives a tribute, as a 'woman of worth', by the recital of the last chapter in the Book of Proverbs.

At least three meals—שָׁלשׁ סְעוּדוֹת—are prescribed by the Rabbis for our enjoyment on Sabbath, at which

זְמִירוֹת (hymns) are sung in praise of God and the Sabbath day. To emphasize the day's joyous spirit, it is customary to wear our finest clothes and to spend a little extra on food. Mourning or fasting are prohibited, so as not to introduce any note of sadness. We can appreciate why the Rabbis call the Sabbath a precious gift. 'The Holy One, blessed be He, said to Moses, I have a precious gift in My treasury, named Sabbath, which I desire to present to Israel. Go and inform them' (*Shabbath* 10 a).

CHAPTER 8

THREE TIMES A YEAR

1 The Three Pilgrim Festivals – Holy Assemblies – The *Eruv* –
Chol Hamoed – *Isru Chag* **2** Passover – The Fast of the First-
born – The Offering of the Paschal Lamb –The Festival of
Unleavened Bread – The Season of our Freedom – The Festival
of Spring **3** The Search for Leaven – The Removal of Leaven –
The *Seder* Service –The *Haggadah* **4** The Synagogue Services –
The Counting of the *Omer* – *Lag Ba'Omer* – *Pesach Sheni*

1 **The Three Pilgrim Festivals:** שָׁלֹשׁ רְגָלִים

*Three times each year shall all your males appear before
the Lord your God in the place which He shall choose, on
the feast of unleavened bread, on the feast of weeks, and
on the feast of tabernacles* (Deut. xvi, 16).

From the time the First Temple was dedicated until the
Second Temple was destroyed in 70 C.E., large numbers
of pilgrims went to Jerusalem on these Festivals from all
parts of the Holy Land and Babylon. They assembled in
the Temple area for prayer, special sacrifices were offered,
and joyful celebrations were held. All three Festivals
commemorate historical events, point the lesson of Divine
Providence and mark important agricultural stages in
the year.

Holy Assemblies: The Torah commands that in *Eretz
Yisrael* the first and seventh days of *Pesach*, the day of
Shavuoth and the first and eighth days of *Succoth* should be
kept as holy assemblies (Lev. xxiii). Outside Israel, as
we have seen above (see p. 52), an additional day is
observed in each case.

60

The Eruv: On these Festival days, just as on the Sabbath, no work may be done, the only exception being that the preparation of food for a particular day of *Yomtov* is permitted. When Sabbath follows immediately after the Holy-day, food may also be cooked for the Sabbath if the preparation was started *before Yomtov* and continued on the Holy-day. To enable us to do so, we prepare on the eve of the Holy-day (*Erev Yomtov*) a symbolic dish which is called עֵרוּב תַּבְשִׁילִין—a mixture or combination of dishes, i.e. of those prepared on the eve of the Festival and those prepared on *Yomtov* itself. An appropriate blessing must be said.

As on *Erev Shabbath*, the candles are kindled at home on *Erev Yomtov* and a blessing is said. *Kiddush* is recited and we insert in the Grace after Meals a paragraph which includes a reference to the particular Festival, known as יַעֲלֶה וְיָבֹא—'May (our remembrance) rise and come (before Thee).' *Havdalah* is said at the end of each Festival, but the blessings over spices and light are not recited on a weekday.

Chol Hamoed: The intermediate days of *Pesach* and *Succoth* are known as חוֹל הַמּוֹעֵד—the secular days of the Festival, in distinction to the Holy-days. They are observed as semi-holy days. Only essential work is permitted, where delay would cause damage. In the Synagogue, *Hallel* and *Musaph* are read in addition to special Readings from the Torah.

Isru Chag: The day after each of the three Festivals is called אִסְרוּ חַג. This literally means 'bind the festival,' and comes from one of the *Hallel* psalms (cxviii 27), *bind the Festival offering with cords even to the horns of the altar. Tachanun* is not said on that day.

Let us now deal with each Festival in turn:

2 **Passover:** פֶּסַח

This Festival is celebrated for eight days (seven in *Israel*), from the 15th to the 22nd of *Nisan*. The Hebrew word *Pesach*, meaning 'passing over,' refers to the smiting of the first-born in Egypt when God 'passed over' the houses of the Children of Israel (Ex. xii, 27), the lintels and door-posts of which had been sprinkled with the blood of the Paschal lamb.

The Fast of the First-born: תַּעֲנִית בְּכוֹרִים. As a token of gratitude for this miraculous deliverance, a fast is observed on *Erev Pesach* by every male first-born. If he participates in the study of the last part of a Talmudic Tractate, it is unnecessary for the first-born to fast. The סִיּוּם (conclusion), as it is called, is celebrated as a festive occasion accompanied by a סְעוּדַת מִצְוָה, i.e. a meal in honour of a religious act, which exempts those taking part from fasting. The *Siyyum* is held in the Synagogue just after the *Shacharith* Service.

The Offering of the Paschal Lamb: קָרְבַּן פֶּסַח. The name *Pesach* is applied to both the Paschal offering and to the Festival as a whole. The sacrifice of the Paschal lamb in Egypt took place on the 14th of *Nisan*. Its flesh was hastily roasted and eaten, together with unleavened bread and bitter herbs, by families waiting for the call to freedom. The command to offer up the *Korban Pesach* was later observed each year in the Temple, the only place where, like all sacrifices, it could be offered up.

The Festival of Unleavened Bread: חַג הַמַּצּוֹת. This is the other name for the Festival mentioned in the Torah and refers to the unleavened bread prepared by the Israelites in their hurried departure from Egypt. In accordance with the Divine command to Moses and Aaron whilst the people were still in Egypt, no leaven was to be eaten in the future during Passover, nor was it to be kept in the house. The term חָמֵץ applies both to bread or any kind of food prepared from the five species of grain (barley, wheat, rye, oats and spelt) which has been allowed to ferment or become leavened.

All vessels used for *chametz* must be stored away, and replaced by others that will be only for Passover. Certain vessels used during the year, can be made *kasher*, i.e. 'fit' for Passover use, after they have been through a special process of cleansing that ensures the removal of every trace of *chametz*. For a proper understanding of this subject careful study should be made of the laws in the *Shulchan Arukh* relating to it.

Although no leaven of any kind may be eaten during *Pesach*, the obligation to eat *Matzah* applies only to the first two nights when, during the *Seder* services, we recite the special blessings. This accords with the command, *In the first month, on the fourteenth day of the month, at even, you shall eat unleavened bread* (Ex. xii, 18).

We must keep in mind the needy who cannot afford to buy the Passover necessities. Many communities arrange a *Matzah* fund to provide the poor with *Matzah*, wine, etc. This is known as מָעוֹת חִטִּין—'money for wheat' —as it was customary for the wheat to be bought by the head of the family and ground into flour, which was then taken to the bakery and made into *Matzah*.

The Season of our Freedom: זְמַן חֵרוּתֵנוּ. The deliverance from Egyptian slavery was a turning point in Israel's history: a new nation was born, to live a life of freedom and independence in the Holy Land and to become devoted to the service of One God. In celebrating the Season of our Freedom, as it is called in our Prayer Books, Israel must never forget its allegiance to God and His Commandments. Indeed the first of the Ten Commandments proclaims God as the Redeemer: *I am the*

Lord your God, who brought you out of the Land of Egypt, out of the house of bondage.

The Festival of Spring: חַג הָאָבִיב. This name is given to *Pesach* because the month of *Nisan* is described in the Torah as the month of *Abib*, when the fresh young ears of barley begin to ripen. Passover is observed as an agricultural festival: in obedience to the Biblical command a measure of barley called an *omer* was brought to the Temple on the second day of Passover in gratitude for God's bounty, and not till this was done could bread made from the new crop be enjoyed.

3 The Search for Leaven: בְּדִיקַת חָמֵץ

To keep scrupulously to the command that 'no leavened bread shall be found in your house' a ceremony is performed at home on the evening before the fourteenth day of *Nisan*: a blessing 'concerning the removal of *chametz*' is recited and a careful search is made for any leaven which may still remain in the house. This takes place at nightfall, and a taper or candle is lit so that breadcrumbs in dark corners may be more easily seen.

The Removal of Leaven: בְּעוּר חָמֵץ. *Chametz* may be eaten on *Erev Pesach* only during the first third of the day. Any leaven remaining must be sold or given to a non-Jew, or destroyed. The morsels of bread collected the previous evening are burnt and a declaration is made by the master of the house in regard to any *chametz* that might still be in the home without his knowledge: 'Let it be annulled and considered as the dust of the earth.'

The Seder Service: And thou shalt tell (vehiggadta) thy son in that day, saying: It is because of that which the Lord did for me when I came forth out of Egypt (Ex. xiii, 8). The duty imposed on the parent by the Torah, to narrate the events of the Exodus to his children every year, has become the central feature of one of the most fascinating of Jewish family celebrations. The *Seder*—סֵדֶר—or Order of Service conducted at home on the first two nights of Passover (only one night in *Israel*) dates back to Temple times. Today's ritual is, with few modifications, the same as the one our ancestors carried out. The Celebrant leans on his left side during the ceremony —the custom of the freeman in ancient times. Symbols placed on the *Seder* table and a special dish remind us of the Egyptian bondage, the Redemption and the Celebration in Temple times.

(i) *Three Matzoth:* They are placed on top of one another, generally in a special cover containing three compartments. The upper and lower *Matzoth* represent the *Lechem Mishneh*, commemorating the double portion of manna provided for the Israelites in the Wilderness on the sixth day of the week and on *Erev Yomtov*. The middle *Matzah*, broken in two at the beginning of the ceremony, represents the לֶחֶם עֹנִי—the 'bread of affliction': the smaller part is eaten in fulfilment of the command to eat *Matzah* (see page 63), and the larger part is set aside for the *Afikoman* (this word is probably derived from the Greek word for 'dessert'). We complete the meal with the *Matzah* of *Afikoman*, recalling Temple times when the meal ended with the eating of the Paschal lamb so that its taste should remain in the mouth. Care is generally taken to obtain מַצָּה שְׁמוּרָה, which has been 'strictly supervised' at every stage in its manufacture— from the cutting of the wheat to the baking—to ensure that no moisture has come into contact with it to cause fermentation.

The three *Matzoth* also represent the three-fold division of the Jewish people—*Cohen*, *Levi* and *Yisrael*.

(ii) *Four Cups of Wine:* אַרְבַּע כּוֹסוֹת: The Mishnah

states that every Jew, however poor, must drink four cups of wine during the *Seder* Service. The first is connected with the recital of *Kiddush*; the second with the story of the Exodus from Egypt and the Blessing for Redemption; the third with the Grace after Meals; and the fourth with the completion of *Hallel* and the prayers for thanksgiving. The four cups also symbolise the four expressions of redemption in Ex. vi, 6 and 7: וְהוֹצֵאתִי, וְגָאַלְתִּי, וְהִצַּלְתִּי, and וְלָקַחְתִּי. *And I shall bring out: And I shall deliver; And I shall redeem* and *And I shall take.*

(iii) *The Cup of Elijah*—כּוֹסוֹ שֶׁל אֵלִיָּהוּ: This cup of wine is a symbol of the hospitality that awaits the passer-by and wayfarer. The Messiah, according to ancient tradition, will reveal himself on Passover, and the Prophet Malachi told that he will be preceded by Elijah. It has also been suggested that the Cup of Elijah was introduced into the *Seder* because of the doubt as to whether five cups of wine should be drunk, in view of the fifth expression of Redemption mentioned in Ex. vi, 8, וְהֵבֵאתִי— 'And I shall bring (you to the Land'.) This, say our Rabbis, together with all other undecided questions of law, are to be left for the consideration of Elijah in time to come.

(iv) *Bitter Herbs*—מָרוֹר: They recall the bitterness of Egyptian slavery.

(v) *Parsley*—כַּרְפַּס (or a similar herb with a pungent flavour): In ancient times vegetables were served as the *hors d'oeuvre* before a meal. The parsley is dipped in salt water and eaten after the recital of the *Kiddush*. This arouses the curiosity of the child at the *Seder* table. Dipping the parsley in the salt water, and later, the bitter herbs in the *Charoseth*, prompt the child to ask, in the *Mah Nishtanah*, 'why the herbs are dipped twice on this night.'

(vi) *Charoseth*—חֲרוֹסֶת: A mixture of apples, nuts, cinnamon and wine: a reminder of the bricks and mortar our ancestors were forced to use when slaves in Egypt. It also serves, the Talmud says, as a protection against any possible ill effects caused by eating bitter herbs.

(vii) *The Roasted Shankbone:* Symbolizing the Paschal offering sacrificed in the Temple on Passover.

(viii) *The Roasted Egg:* Commemorating the *Chagigah*, the Festival sacrifice offered in the Temple, which was added to the Paschal offering when the company was large.

(ix) *Salt Water:* This is probably meant to recall that salt was offered with all sacrifices in the Temple, the *Seder* being the symbolic reminder of the *Korban Pesach*. Another suggestion is that we are thus reminded by the salt water of the tears shed by our ancestors in Egypt.

The Haggadah—הַגָּדָה. The *Haggadah* booklet is designed especially for the younger generation, in accordance with the Biblical command (Ex. xiii, 8). Our Rabbis were aware that the child's interest must be stimulated and that he must be made to feel he is taking an active part in the *Seder* ceremony; so it is the principle of 'learning by doing' which underlies their idea of giving to the child such an important place in the Passover ceremonies. The order of the Service is given in most editions of the *Haggadah* in rhyme, as follows:

(i)   קַדֵּשׁ The *Kiddush* is recited.

(ii)   וּרְחַץ The Celebrant washes his hands before eating the vegetables.

(iii)   כַּרְפַּס The parsley is dipped in salt water after the recital of the Blessing over vegetables.

(iv)   יַחַץ The Celebrant 'divides' the middle *Matzah*, laying aside the larger part for the *Afikoman*.

(v)   מַגִּיד   The narration of the *Haggadah*.

(vi)   רָחְצָה   Each participant washes his hands, before the meal.

(vii)   מוֹצִיא   Blessing over bread, recited because the *Matzah* represents the bread eaten at ordinary meals.

(viii)   מַצָּה   Blessing over *Matzah*.

(ix)   מָרוֹר   Bitter herbs are eaten after the appropriate blessing has been recited.

(x)   כּוֹרֵךְ   'Combining' the *Matzah* and *Maror*, just as Hillel did in Temple times.

(xi)   שֻׁלְחָן עוֹרֵךְ   'The table is laid'—i.e. the evening meal is eaten.

(xii)   צָפוּן   'Laid aside'—the *Afikoman* is eaten.

(xiii)   בָּרֵךְ   Grace after Meals is recited.

(xiv)   הַלֵּל   The *Hallel* is completed.

(xv)   נִרְצָה   'Accepted,' i.e. may our service be acceptable to God.

The *Haggadah* ends with several hymns and songs designed for the special enjoyment of children.

4 The Synagogue Services

The מַחְזוֹר—lit. 'cycle' (of prayers), the Festival Prayer Book—contains the Prayers and Portions of the Law and Prophets prescribed for the eight days of the Festival. In the main, they refer to the departure from Egypt, the crossing of the Red Sea and the celebration of the Passover. Because the rainy period in Israel ends early in *Nisan*, a prayer for dew—תְּפִלַת טַל—is offered on the first day of the Festival during the *Musaph* Service. On *Pesach*, the Rabbis tell us, the world is judged for produce (*Rosh Hashanah* i, 2). The occasion being a solemn one, the Reader wears the white *Kittel* or robe—a symbol of purity and humility—as on *Rosh Hashanah* and *Yom Kippur*. With the approach of the summer the descent of dew is one of the greatest blessings which can come to the farmer in Israel.

On *Shabbath Chol Hamoed*, or on the Seventh or the Eighth day, if either falls on a Sabbath, the Song of Songs—one of the five *Megilloth*—is read. As already mentioned (p. 27), this love song between a shepherd and shepherdess is regarded by some Rabbis as meaning God's love for Israel, whom he redeemed from Egypt. Furthermore, the scene in the book is set against the background of the Spring, when *the flowers appear on the earth, the time of singing has come and the voice of the turtledove is heard in our land* (ii, 12).

The Counting of the Omer: סְפִירַת הָעֹמֶר. *And you shall count unto you from the morrow after the day of rest, from the day that you brought the sheaf of the waving: seven weeks shall there be complete* (Lev. xxiii, 15). The Israelites were in this way commanded to count forty-nine days from the second day of *Pesach*, when the *Omer* was brought to the Temple, the fiftieth day being celebrated as the wheat harvest—the Festival of *Shavuoth*. After Temple times the *Omer* could no longer be offered up, but the counting of the days at nightfall continued to be strictly observed.

Lag Ba'Omer: The period between *Pesach* and *Shavuoth* has often been a most unfortunate one for our people. In the days of Rabbi Akiba a devastating plague broke out among his disciples and ceased only on the 18th of *Iyyar*, the 33rd day of the *Omer*—לַ״ג בָּעֹמֶר—which became known as the Scholar's Feast. During the Crusades thousands of Jews were massacred at this time of the year. It is for this reason that during the whole month of *Iyyar*, with the exception of *Lag Ba'Omer*, no weddings or other joyous occasions are celebrated.

Lag Ba'Omer itself is a day of joy, especially in *Eretz Yisrael*. Masses of people make their way to Meron in the hills of Safed, where Simeon ben Yochai is buried. He was a disciple of R. Akiba, and, defying the cruel decrees of Hadrian, continued to teach his students the Torah. He escaped from the Romans with his son and hid in a cave in the Galilee hills for thirteen years. Legend has it that Elijah appeared before them to tell them of the Roman Emperor's death, and then R. Simeon settled in Meron and continued his sacred task until he died on *Lag Ba'Omer*.

Pesach Sheni: פֶּסַח שֵׁנִי. As we have seen, the Paschal lamb was to be sacrificed only in the Temple on the 14th of *Nisan*. Those who were in a state of impurity or a long way from home could not take part, but they were permitted to make the offering a month later on the 14th of *Iyyar* (Num. ix, 9-12). To distinguish it from the former the sacrifice was called 'the Second Passover'.

CHAPTER 9

THREE TIMES A YEAR

(continued)

1 *Shavuoth* – The Festival of the Wheat Harvest – The Day of First-fruits 2 The Season of the Giving of our Law – The Synagogue Services – The Three Days of Bordering 3 *Succoth* – The Festival of the Ingathering – The *arbaah minim* 4 The Season of our Rejoicing 5 *Hoshana Rabba* 6 *Shemini Atzereth* 7 *Simchath Torah*

1 **Shavuoth:** שָׁבוּעוֹת

This Festival is celebrated for two days (one day in *Israel*), on the 6th and 7th of *Sivan*. *Shavuoth* means 'weeks': seven weeks are counted from the bringing of the *Omer* on the second day of *Pesach* (Lev. xxiii, 15). *Shavuoth* is on the 50th day and its name of 'Pentecost' is a Greek word meaning 'fiftieth.' In the Bible it is also known by two other names.

(i) *The Festival of the Wheat Harvest*—חַג הַקָּצִיר. In Biblical times *Shavuoth* was, in the main, a harvest festival. On the fiftieth day after the bringing of the *Omer*, the start of the wheat harvest was celebrated by a thanksgiving offering of two loaves made from the new crop.

(ii) *The Day of First-fruits*—יוֹם הַבִּכּוּרִים. From this day until the Festival of *Succoth* the first-fruits of the field (wheat, barley, grapes, figs, pomegranates, olives and date-honey) were brought by the farmer to the Temple as tokens of gratitude to the Almighty for His blessings. The Mishnah *Bikkurim* describes the colourful ceremonies.

71

After selecting the first-fruits from the best produce, the farmers placed them in ornamental baskets and carried them to Jerusalem. As they approached the city they were welcomed in joy by the chief officials of the Temple, and on arriving at the Temple each man recited the passage in Deuteronomy xxvi, 5, beginning with the words 'A wandering Aramean was my father.' He then left his basket of fruit at the side of the Altar, bowed and departed.

The agricultural nature of the Festival is nowadays represented by the beautiful flowers and large plants with which the Synagogue is adorned. These also remind us of the statement in the Mishnah that on *Shavuoth* the world is judged in the matter of the fruits of trees, i.e. judgment is made as to whether we deserve an abundant fruit harvest or not (*Rosh Hashanah* i, 2).

2 The Season of the Giving of Our Law: זְמַן מַתַּן תּוֹרָתֵנוּ

The Revelation at Mount Sinai, the Bible tells us, came in the third month after the Exodus, i.e. in *Sivan*. Our Rabbis, after careful consideration of the relevant passages prove that the anniversary falls on the sixth day of the month. *Shavuoth* thus celebrates the day when Israel undertook allegiance to the laws of God.

In the Talmud the Festival is also called עֲצֶרֶת, meaning 'conclusion,' as it ends the period of seven weeks counted from the second day of *Pesach*.

The Synagogue Services: Prayers and poems are recited at the Synagogue services referring both to the Divine revelation and to the blessings of nature. On the first day the Reading of the Law (Ex. xix and xx) includes the passage containing the Ten Commandments. *Megillath* Ruth is read on the second day for three reasons: (*a*) it gives an account of the Harvest and of kind treatment of the poor, (*b*) it relates the acceptance by Ruth of the Jewish faith, and (*c*) Ruth was the ancestress of King David who, according to tradition, died on *Shavuoth*.

The Three Days of Bordering: שְׁלֹשֶׁת יְמֵי הַגְבָּלָה. From the 3rd to the 5th of *Sivan*, the Israelites, told to prepare themselves for the Great Event, were forbidden to ascend Mount Sinai or touch its border (Ex. xix, 10-12). These three days are known as 'The Three Days of Bordering'. It is the custom to spend the first night of *Shavuoth* in the study of a special anthology of Biblical and Talmudical passages, preparing ourselves, as it were, for the Giving of the Law. This book is known as תִּקוּן לֵיל שָׁבוּעוֹת — 'preparation for *Shavuoth* night.'

3 Succoth: סֻכּוֹת

On the fifteenth day of this seventh month and for seven days is the feast of Tabernacles to the Lord (Lev. xxiii, 34). This Festival, therefore, starting on the 15th of *Tishri*, commemorates the Divine Protection given to the Israelites during their wanderings through the wilderness. *You shall dwell in booths for seven days . . . that your generations may know that I made the people of Israel dwell in booths when I brought them out of the land of Egypt* (Lev. xxiii, 42 and 43). The *Succah*, a frail and temporary booth, could hardly have provided enough safety from danger in the desert without God's protection.

For this reason we build our *Succah*, eat our meals in it and, if possible, sleep there at night, expressing our complete trust and confidence in God. The *Shulchan Arukh* sets out the laws of erecting the *Succah* so as to ensure that it is a temporary structure. Its roof, for example, must be covered only with detached branches of trees, plants and leaves, leaving gaps through which the stars can be seen.

The Festival of The Ingathering: חַג הָאָסִיף. The other name given to this festival in the Torah refers to the gathering of produce from the fields in autumn. It was an important agricultural occasion and a time for rejoicing. *And you shall take, on the first day, the fruit of goodly trees, branches of palm trees and boughs of leafy trees and willows of the brook; and you shall rejoice before the Lord your God seven days* (Lev. xxiii, 40).

In Synagogue we observe the commandment by taking in our hand the אַרְבָּעָה מִינִים—the four species consisting of the palm branch-לוּלָב; three myrtle branches-הֲדַסִּים; two branches of the willow—עֲרָבוֹת; and the citron —אֶתְרוֹג. The blessing we recite mentions the *Lulav*, which is the largest of the four species.

On each day of the Festival, with the exception of Sabbath, we take the *Lulav* before and during the recital of *Hallel* and wave it in every direction, symbolizing God's sovereignty over the whole world. Holding the four species, we make one circuit—הַקָּפָה—round the *Sepher Torah*, which is carried on to the *Bimah*, on each of the first six days. During the circuit, the *Hoshana* prayers are recited, each ending with the word *Hoshana*, 'save us.' This is based on the practice followed in Temple times when the *Lulav* was waved and the priests made a circuit round the Altar, decorated with willow branches, singing parts of the *Hallel*. The *Lulav* is not used on the Sabbath as it might have to be carried from place to place through the public thoroughfare—which is forbidden on Sabbath.

In the Bible and Talmud, the festival is also known simply as חַג—'Feast'. In our Prayer Books it is described as 'The Season of our Rejoicing'.

4 The Season of our Rejoicing: זְמַן שִׂמְחָתֵנוּ

The joyful ceremonial of the Festival reached its climax in Temple times when the procedure known as 'The joy of the Water-Drawing'—שִׂמְחַת בֵּית הַשּׁוֹאֵבָה—began on the second night of *Succoth* and lasted for six days. Each morning a libation offering of water was made. It was taken in a golden ewer from the pool of Siloam, carried with great pomp and ceremony, and was poured into a perforated silver bowl placed on the west side of the Altar, symbolizing the abundant rain for which the people prayed. Bonfires were lit and men of piety danced, holding lighted torches and singing songs and hymns to the accompaniment of harps, lyres, cymbals and trumpets, played by the Levites. We can well understand the statement in the Mishnah, 'He who has never witnessed the rejoicing at the ceremony of water-drawing has never seen real joy in his life' (*Succah* v, 1).

5 Hoshana Rabba: הוֹשַׁעֲנָא רַבָּא

'The Great Hoshana' is the name given to the seventh day of *Succoth* because of the seven circuits—הַקָּפוֹת—we make round the *Siphre Torah* while reciting a large number of the *Hoshana* prayers. In Mishnaic times, this day was known as 'the day of the willow branch'. After the priests had completed their seven circuits round the Altar, they beat the willow branches on the ground. It is on this ceremony that our present custom is based. It symbolizes the end of one season and the renewal of another. We pray that God will send rain and dew to produce fresh leaves and, as it were, renew our own strength in the coming year. In the course of time, *Hoshana Rabba* came to be regarded as the day when Divine judgment was to be given. The Service is therefore conducted with solemnity and the Reader puts on the white *Kittel* (see p. 69). The pious spend the night reading the Book of Deuteronomy and selections from the Bible and Mishnah, contained in a *Tikkun* (see p. 73).

6 Shemini Atzereth: שְׁמִינִי עֲצֶרֶת

On the eighth day you shall hold a holy convocation . . . it is a day of solemn assembly (Lev. xxiii, 36). In *Israel*, *Shemini Atzereth and Simchath Torah* are celebrated on the one day; in the Diaspora each is observed on a separate day. Both are holy days and no work is permitted. On *Shemini Atzereth*, a prayer for rain—תְּפִלַּת גֶּשֶׁם—is offered up. Our Rabbis tell us that this is the season when the world is judged for water (*Rosh Hashanah* i, 2), and the Reader again wears his white *Kittel*. The words — מַשִּׁיב הָרוּחַ וּמוֹרִיד הַגֶּשֶׁם — 'You cause the wind to blow and the rain to fall' are inserted in the second paragraph of the *Amidah* from *Shemini Atzereth* until the first day of *Pesach*.

Megillath Koheleth is read at the end of the Morning Service on *Shabbath Chol Hamoed* or on *Shemini Atzereth* if it falls on the Sabbath. In the midst of our rejoicing it is well to ponder on the more serious aspects of life, which King Solomon describes in this book (see p. 27).

7 Simchath Torah: שִׂמְחַת תּוֹרָה

On the ninth day of *Succoth*, the festivity called by the name 'Rejoicing of the Law' is celebrated. On it, we complete and re-commence the annual reading of the Torah. It is a joyous occasion on which the *Siphre Torah* are taken out of the Ark, and the members of the congregation carry them in procession round the Synagogue. Children, too, play a part in the ceremonies. There is the happy custom of all boys under thirteen—כָּל

הַנְּעָרִים—being called up together to the Reading of the Torah together with an adult who recites the Blessings. Special honours are given to two worthy members of the congregation: they are called up to the reading of the concluding portion and the first portion of the Torah, respectively. The first is known as the חֲתַן תּוֹרָה—Bridegroom of the Law, and the second as the חֲתַן בְּרֵאשִׁית—Bridegroom of *Bereshith*.

CHAPTER 10

TEN DAYS OF SOLEMNITY

1 **The Yamim Noraim:** יָמִים נוֹרָאִים

Beginning with *Rosh Hashanah*, on the first of *Tishri*,
and ending with *Yom Kippur*, on the tenth of the month,
the Jewish year's most solemn and awe-inspiring days are
observed. Known also as the ten days of repentance—
עֲשֶׂרֶת יְמֵי תְשׁוּבָה—they give each one of us the oppor-
tunity to think about our conduct during the year, and to
ask forgiveness for any sins we may have committed
against God and man.

Unlike the three Pilgrim Festivals, neither *Rosh
Hashanah* nor *Yom Kippur* celebrates an agricultural or
historical occasion, but is purely religious in character.
Yet these are not days of sadness or mourning but rather
of comfort and hope. We are confident that God in His
Justice will be merciful to those who are truly repentant
and return to Him. Prayer, charity and repentance, say
our Rabbis, can annul evil decrees (*Bereshith Rabbah*
xliv, 12). Elsewhere we read: Better is one hour of
repentance and good deeds in this world than the whole
life of the World to Come (*Avoth* iv, 22).

The Torah commands the keeping of *Rosh Hashanah*
and *Yom Kippur* as Holy Assemblies, when no work is
permitted. On *Rosh Hashanah*, just as with the three

Pilgrim Festivals, food may be prepared for the particular day of the *Yomtov*. If the first day falls on a Thursday, the *Eruv Tavshilin* must then be prepared (see p. 61), since the Sabbath falls immediately after the holy days. On *Rosh Hashanah*, the candles are lit at home, the *Lechem Mishneh* is placed on the table and *Kiddush* is recited. Just before the beginning of *Yom Kippur*, which is a fast day, the candles only are lit at home before we go to the Synagogue.

The Month of Elul: There is a tradition that Moses ascended Mount Sinai for the third time, on the first of *Elul* to pray that Israel's sin of making the Golden Calf be forgiven. He returned to the people on the tenth of *Tishri* bringing with him the message of Divine pardon. *Elul* is therefore observed as a month of preparation so that we can think hard about the meaning of the Solemn Days that are approaching. The *shophar* is sounded on weekdays at the end of the *Shacharith* Service and special prayers for forgiveness—סְלִיחוֹת—are recited at dawn, in most communities from the Sunday before *Rosh Hashanah*, until *Yom Kippur*. When *Rosh Hashanah* falls on a Monday or Tuesday, the recital of *Selichoth* begins on the second Sunday before the Festival.

2 Rosh Hashanah: רֹאשׁ הַשָּׁנָה

In the seventh month on the first day of the month shall be a solemn rest to you (Lev. xxiii, 24).

The Festival of the New Year is celebrated even in *Israel* for two days, on the first and second of *Tishri* (see p. 52). In the Bible, the names given to this festival are 'The day of sounding the *shophar*'—יוֹם תְּרוּעָה—and the 'Memorial of the blowing of the *shophar*'—זִכְרוֹן תְּרוּעָה. It is also called, in our prayers, 'The Day of

Memorial'—יוֹם הַזִּכָּרוֹן—and 'The Day of Judgment'—
יוֹם הַדִּין. According to rabbinic tradition, the world was
created on the first day of *Tishri*; and in a number of our
prayers we proclaim God as the Creator and King of the
Universe.

To usher in the New Year it is customary, after
Kiddush, to eat apple dipped in honey—symbolizing our
hopes for a sweet and happy year. The standard greeting
is: לְשָׁנָה טוֹבָה תִּכָּתֵבוּ 'May you be inscribed (in the Book
of Life) for a Happy Year.'

The Shophar: The central feature of the *Rosh Hashanah*
Services is the sound of the *shophar*, a ram's horn. The
sound was heard on many important occasions in Biblical
times. Its shrill tone accompanied the Revelation on
Mount Sinai; it warned people that a battle was approaching or proclaimed that hostilities had stopped. Isaiah and
Zechariah prophesied that this sound will precede the
gathering together of the exiles and the Messianic Age.
The *shophar* at New Year time warns us to reflect on our
deeds and ask forgiveness from God, the Creator, who
gave us the Torah. He will surely hear our pleas and
grant peace to the House of Israel.

Writing on the message which the *shophar* brings,
Maimonides advises us: 'Awake from your slumbers
and ponder your deeds. Remember your Creator . . . look
well to your souls and consider your actions. Forsake
each one of you your evil thoughts and ways and return
to God so that He may have mercy upon you.'

This ram's horn which is blown in our Synagogue,
recalls the *Akedah*, or 'Binding' of Isaac, when a ram
was offered up in his stead. That event occurred on *Rosh
Hashanah*, according to tradition. If *Rosh Hashanah* falls
on a Sabbath, the *shophar* is not blown, as it might have
to be carried from place to place through the public

thoroughfare—an act forbidden on the Sabbath Day.

The Day of Memorial: When we remember our conduct during the past year, we realise our weaknesses and approach God with a repentant heart. We pray, too, that He will remember the pious deeds of our ancestors and, for their sakes, show mercy towards us.

The Day of Judgment: As the Children of God we must account to Him for the way we spend our lives. On this day, in the words of the Mishnah, we pass before Him for judgment (*Rosh Hashanah* i, 2). Our sincere intention to follow in His paths and lead a good life will find favour in His sight, we firmly believe, so that we may be inscribed in the Book of Life.

The Synagogue Services: The *Amidah* of the *Musaph* Service, is the longest in our Prayer Book. Its three main sections illustrate the fundamental teachings of *Rosh Hashanah*: GOD'S SOVEREIGNTY, HIS PROVIDENCE and REVELATION. The texts are known respectively as: (*a*) מַלְכִיּוֹת—dealing with God's Sovereignty, and introduced by the *Alenu* prayer (see p. 46); (*b*) זִכְרוֹנוֹת—God's remembrance when He judges us of the acts of faith performed by our ancestors; and (*c*) שׁוֹפָרוֹת—verses relating to the *shophar*, with special emphasis on the Revelation on Sinai and the Messianic Age. Each introductory section is followed by ten biblical verses; three from the Torah, three from the Holy Writings, three from the Prophets, and another from the Torah. The *Gemara* points out that this number corresponds to the Ten Commandments.

The Readings from the Torah on the first and second days relate, respectively, to the birth of Isaac and the *Akedah*. The *Haphtarah* (I Samuel i.1-ii, 10) on the first day deals with the birth of Samuel who was later to dedicate his life to the Service of God. On the second day we read the prophecy of Jeremiah (xxxi, 2-20), foretelling the restoration of Israel.

A hundred notes in all are blown on the *shophar* at three periods during the Service: thirty immediately after the Reading of the Law; thirty during *Musaph* (ten at the end of each of the three main sections); thirty after *Musaph*; and a final ten before *Alenu*. As we are uncertain about the exact tone of the *teruah* prescribed by Jewish Law, we have three variants: תְּקִיעָה—the 'plain' note with an abrupt ending; שְׁבָרִים—'broken' notes, and תְּרוּעָה—a 'wavering' sound.

Tashlich: תַּשְׁלִיךְ (lit. 'you shall cast'): The custom of going to the sea-shore or the banks of a river on the afternoon of the first day began about the fifteenth century. If the day falls on Sabbath we go on the second day of the Festival. The prayers we say and the three verses we quote from the Book of Micah (vii, 18-20) express confidence in the Divine forgiveness. The term *Tashlich* is taken from verse 19, *And you will cast all their sins into the depths of the sea.*

3 Ten Days of Repentance

During the ten days we insert in the services a number of prayers, one of the most important being the אָבִינוּ מַלְכֵּנוּ 'O, our Father, O our King'. The basis of this prayer of forty-four verses is to be found in the Talmud; some of the lines we recite were uttered by R. Akiba on a fast day in time of drought. Other lines were added in later centuries, evidently in periods of persecution and danger. They stress the theme of repentance.

The Sabbath between *Rosh Hashanah* and *Yom Kippur* is known as שַׁבָּת שׁוּבָה—The Sabbath of 'Return,' since the day's *Haphtarah* begins with the words of

Hosea, *Return* (O Israel, to the Lord your God) (Hosea xiv, 2).

4 Yom Kippur: יוֹם כִּפּוּר

On the tenth day of this seventh month is the Day of Atonement; there shall be a holy convocation unto you and you shall afflict your souls . . . It shall be unto you a sabbath of solemn rest and you shall afflict your souls; on the ninth day of the month at even from even to even (Lev. xxiii, 27 and 32).

On *Yom Kippur*, the most solemn day of the Jewish Year, we obey this command to afflict our souls by fasting, from the evening of the ninth of *Tishri* to nightfall on the following day. The period is spent in continuous prayer for forgiveness, so that we may be cleansed of our sins. Fasting in itself cannot secure God's forgiveness; it must be accompanied by sincere repentance, and a firm resolve to make amends for the past and lead a noble life in the future. Nor must we think that *Yom Kippur* will automatically bring forgiveness. The Mishnah (*Yoma* viii, 9) tells us that 'when a person says I shall sin and *Yom Kippur* will procure forgiveness, *Yom Kippur* will not procure forgiveness.' Furthermore, 'it is only for the transgressions against God that *Yom Kippur* atones, but as for transgressions against our neighbour, there can be no atonement until we have first righted any wrongs we may have committed.'

The Synagogue Services: There are five special Services during the day. In them we make confession of our sins—וִדּוּי—in two prayers that are arranged alphabetically. These begin with the words, אָשַׁמְנוּ—'we have trespassed,' and עַל חֵטְא—'for the sin' (we have committed before Thee). The plural 'we' is used throughout: the individual may not have committed the sins listed but he expresses regret that others have done so and that he has not been able to prevent them.

The five Services are:

(i) *Kol Nidre:* כָּל נִדְרֵי (lit. 'all the vows'). The *Maariv* Service on the evening of the Fast Day is so called because the opening prayer begins with these words. In an atmosphere of great solemnity, we plead to God to absolve us from any vows we may voluntarily make to Him but which we do not fulfil. The prayer does *not* refer to obligations we may undertake towards our neighbour. If these are not fulfilled we must approach him personally and obtain his pardon. For the *Kol Nidre* service, male members of the congregation wear the *Tallith*, the praying-shawl that is usually worn only for morning services.

(ii) and (iii) *Shacharith and Musaph:* The Readings of the Torah during the *Shacharith* Service describe the ceremony of purification in the Sanctuary and the sacrifices offered on *Yom Kippur*. The *Haphtarah*, taken from Isaiah lvii, 14-lviii, 14, emphasizes one of the real purposes of fasting: *Is not this the fast that I have chosen? —to loose the fetters of wickedness . . . Is it not to deal your bread to the hungry and that you bring the poor that are cast out to your house? When you see the naked that you cover him, and that you hide not yourself from your own flesh?* One of the main features of the *Musaph* Service is the עֲבוֹדָה, i.e. the service in the Temple conducted by the High Priest. Three times on the Day of Atonement the High Priest made a confession of sins on behalf of himself and his family, the priests and the whole House of Israel. The ancient ceremonies are graphically described in the prayers.

(iv) *Minchah:* The importance of leading a pure family life is emphasized by the Reading of the Law, taken from

Lev. xviii, dealing with forbidden marriages. For the *Haphtarah*, we read the Book of Jonah which teaches that repentance by Jew and non-Jew alike will gain the forgiveness of God.

(v) נְעִילָה—lit., 'The Closing' (of the Gates of Heaven) or, as some suggest, of the Gates of the Temple in the evening, when special prayers were recited. After a day spent in fasting and supplication, we make a final plea to God: to *seal* us in the Book of Life and to answer our prayers.

Neilah ends with the recitation of the first verse of the *Shema*, followed by 'Blessed be His name, whose glorious Kingdom is for ever and ever,' and the words 'The Lord, He is God,' uttered by Israel at Mount Carmel when they witnessed the triumph of Elijah over the prophets of Baal. The single sound of the *shophar* proclaims the end of the Holy Day.

DAYS OF JOY

So far, we have dealt with those festivals which the Torah commands us to keep as holy days, when no kind of work is permitted. There are also in the Jewish calendar a number of joyful days when we are allowed to follow our daily tasks. In the Synagogue Services on these days we omit the *Tachanun* prayers (see p. 45).

1 **Chanucah:** חֲנֻכָּה—(the Festival of) 'Re-dedication'

This Festival is celebrated for eight days from the 25th of *Kislev*. It commemorates the re-dedication of the Temple by Judas Maccabeus and his followers after they defeated the Syrians in 165 B.C.E.

When Alexander the Great conquered Persia in 333 B.C.E., Palestine, which was under Persian rule, became part of the Greek Empire. After Alexander's death, a year later, his empire was divided and Palestine became subject to Egypt and later to Syria. The Jews were, in general, able to organize their religious life without interference; but when Antiochus Epiphanes (i.e. the illustrious), became King of Syria in 175 B.C.E., he tried hard to make them accept Hellenism, as the old Greek way of life was called. He ordered them to worship Greek gods, and forbade the practice of Judaism under penalty of death.

86

On the 25th of *Kislev*, in the year 168 B.C.E., a sacrifice of swine flesh was offered on the holy altar of the Temple, which Antiochus dedicated to Zeus. In the Judean town of Modin the priest, Mattathias the Hasmonean, decided, with his five sons, to oppose the king and, joined by small bands of loyal Jews, they led an uprising against him. Mattathias died, but his son Judah took command and after three years of fighting the enemy was overthrown.

On the 25th of *Kislev*, exactly three years after the desecration of the altar, Judah entered the Temple with his followers and re-dedicated it to God's service. His courage won him the title of Maccabee, which probably comes from a Hebrew word meaning the 'hammerer.' It is also suggested that the Hebrew form of the word— מַכַּבִּי—is made up of the first letters of the motto inscribed on his banner— מִי כָמוֹךָ בָּאֵלִים יי —'*Who is like unto Thee, O Lord, among the mighty?*' (Ex. xv, 11).

The Festival of Lights: Chanucah is known also as חַג הָאוּרִים—the Festival of Lights. When the Hasmoneans entered the Temple, the Talmud says, they found that only one cruse of oil remained which had not been defiled by the heathen—the seal of the High Priest was unbroken. This would have been enough to keep the *Menorah* (Candelabrum) alight for only a day. But, miraculously, the oil lasted eight days. Therefore, we are told, these days were appointed as a Festival, and both in Synagogue and at home we kindle *Menorah* lights during *Chanucah's* eight days. Following the principles laid down by *Beth Hillel*, we light one candle on the first night, two on the second night, and so on. As we are not allowed to make secular use of the *Chanucah* lights, we add the שַׁמָּשׁ—the 'attendant light,' so that if we have to carry out any task near the *Menorah*, we are, as it were, using the light of the *Shamash*.

87

The two blessings recited before kindling the lights are both mentioned in the Talmud. The first ends with the words: 'Who has commanded us to kindle the light of *Chanucah*,' and the second with: 'Who performed miracles for our fathers in days of old at this season.' On the first night the blessing *Shehecheyanu* is also said.

The Synagogue Services: The complete *Hallel* is recited each day during *Shacharith*. The Readings from the Torah, taken from Numbers vii, deal with the daily gifts offered by the princes of the twelve tribes at the dedication of the altar in the wilderness, and the kindling of the *Menorah* in the Sanctuary. The *Haphtarah* on *Shabbath* (Zechariah ii, 14-iv, 7) includes the famous message of the prophet, assuring the people that God will help them in their task of re-building the Temple—*Not by might, nor by power, but by My spirit, saith the Lord of Hosts*. If there is a second *Shabbath Chanucah*, the *Haphtarah* is taken from the First Book of Kings vii, 40-50, where the gifts and utensils made for the first Temple in Solomon's reign are described.

A paragraph is inserted in the *Amidah* and Grace after Meals beginning with the words עַל הַנִּסִּים—'for the miracles, etc.' This gives a brief account of the *Chanucah* story, when God, in His abundant mercy, 'delivered the strong into the hands of the weak and the many into the hands of the few.'

2 Purim: פּוּרִים

The Feast of Lots is celebrated on the 14th of *Adar*, or of *Adar Sheni* in a leap year. The word *Purim* means 'lots,' cast by Haman to decide the month he thought most favourable for exterminating the Jews in Persia. The 13th of *Adar* is observed as a minor fast, for it was the day on which Haman's plot was to be carried out:

the Jews repelled the enemy and celebrated their deliverance on the following day. The fast is called תַּעֲנִית אֶסְתֵּר—the Fast of Esther—as Queen Esther fasted for three days before approaching Ahasuerus to ask him to revoke the evil decree. For the Scriptural passages read on this day, see p. 95.

The Synagogue Services: Both at the evening and the morning service of the 14th day of *Adar*, we read the *Megillath Esther*—which is known as THE *Megillah*, and is preceded by three Blessings alluded to in the Talmud: 'Who has commanded us concerning the Reading of the *Megillah*';—'Who performed miracles for our fathers in days of old at this season'; and *Shehecheyanu*. After the reading of the *Megillah*, another Blessing is said praising God for punishing the foes of Israel. The regulations governing the writing of the *Megillah* are similar to those of the *Sepher Torah*: it must be written on specially prepared parchment, in ink, and in square Hebrew characters.

We read that Mordecai sent a letter to all the Jews after their deliverance (Ch. ix, 26). The Synagogue Reader, therefore, spreads out the *Megillah* and folds it folio by folio, as though it were written in the form of a long letter. For the Reading from the Torah in the *Shacharith* Service, we take the passage relating to the war with Amalek—Haman's remote ancestor (Ex. xvii, 8-16). The paragraph *Al Hanissim*, inserted in the *Amidah* and Grace after Meals, proclaims the Divine deliverance from the enemy.

Just as was done in the days of Mordecai and Esther, the occasion is celebrated by the sending of gifts to friends—מִשְׁלוֹחַ מָנוֹת—and by providing gifts for the poor—מַתָּנוֹת לָאֶבְיוֹנִים. A special סְעוּדָה or festive meal is enjoyed in the afternoon. It is also customary to contribute 'half a shekel'—מַחֲצִית הַשֶּׁקֶל—for the poor before the reading of the *Megillah*. In Temple times, every male over the age of twenty gave this amount towards the upkeep of the Temple and its sacrifices, and it had to be paid during *Adar* (see p. 99).

Shushan Purim: The 15th of *Adar* is called *Shushan Purim*—שׁוּשַׁן פּוּרִים. The Jews of Shushan, the capital of Persia, continued the attack on the enemy on the 14th of *Adar* and celebrated their victory on the 15th. Our Rabbis ruled that those cities which, like Shushan, had ancient walls dating back to the days of Joshua, should celebrate *Purim* on the 15th of *Adar*. For this reason *Purim* is celebrated in Jerusalem, which had a wall in the days of Joshua, on the 15th of *Adar*, whereas in a modern city like Tel-Aviv the celebration is on the 14th.

In a leap year, when *Purim* is celebrated in *Adar Sheni*, the 14th and 15th of *Adar Rishon* are called פּוּרִים קָטָן— 'the minor Purim.'

3 **Rosh Chodesh:** רֹאשׁ חֹדֶשׁ (lit. 'the head of the month').

It is clear from several passages in the Bible that *Rosh Chodesh* was at one time an established Festival, and, as on the Sabbath and Festivals an additional sacrifice was offered. When the Shunamite woman wished to visit Elisha after her son appeared to have died, her husband asks, *Why will you go to him today? It is neither New Moon nor Sabbath* (II Kings iv, 23). The Prophet Amos denounces the evil-doers who say, *When will the New Moon be over that we may sell grain, and the Sabbath that we may offer wheat for sale?* (viii, 5). This seems to indicate that at one time no work was allowed on *Rosh Chodesh*.

The Rabbis later allowed work to be done on *Rosh Chodesh*, but it was still observed as a minor Festival. During the *Shacharith* Service, 'half' *Hallel* is said; there is a Reading from the Law, taken from Numbers (xxviii, 1-15), which deals with the sacrificial offering of the day, and a special *Musaph* is recited. In every *Amidah* (apart from *Musaph*) and in the Grace after Meals, the prayer יַעֲלֶה וְיָבֹא (see p. 61) is added.

4 The New Year for Trees: רֹאשׁ הַשָּׁנָה לָאִילָנוֹת

It was ruled by *Beth Hillel*, that the 15th of *Shevat* be declared the New Year for Trees. In the year which followed, the various tithes of the fruit produced during the period had to be set aside by the owner. The day marks the end of the heavy-rain season in Palestine, when the new sap starts to rise in the trees. After the destruction of the Temple, when the tithe laws could no longer be applied, a number of customs based purely on the day's agricultural significance were observed. In the sixteenth and seventeenth centuries, the mystic sect known as the Cabalists, who settled in Palestine, partook of fifteen kinds of fruit on that day the 15th of *Shevat*. In recent years, in *Eretz Yisrael* particularly, ט״ו בִּשְׁבָט, as it is called, has become one of the year's happiest days. Schoolchildren plant thousands of saplings in the hills and vales—recalling the words of the Torah, *When you come into the land you shall plant all kinds of trees* (Lev. xix, 23).

5 The 15th of Av: חֲמִשָּׁה עָשָׂר בְּאָב

In Temple times, wood was brought for the burning of the sacrifices at certain periods of the year. The 15th of *Av* was Midsummer Day, when, because of the great heat, the people stopped hewing wood in the forest, and all of them, together with the priests, took part in this wood offering. It was a day of jollity, the Talmud says, when the young maidens of Jerusalem, dressed in white, went out to the vineyards to dance—and then the young men were invited to choose their brides. The *Gemara* tells of several events which occurred on the 15th of *Av*: the tribe of Benjamin were reconciled with the other Israelites, after their bitter quarrel (Judges xxi): the generation of Israelites wandering in the wilderness ceased to die off; the guards appointed by Jeroboam, who had made two golden calfs in Dan and Bethel to prevent the people going to Jerusalem on pilgrimage, were removed; and permission was given to bury the dead of Bethar, after the storming of the city in the time of Bar Cochba.

6 Independence Day: יוֹם הָעַצְמָאוּת

Throughout the centuries Jews have prayed for Zion and Jerusalem to be restored to their ancient glory. Towards the end of the nineteenth century their hopes began to be realised when the first Palestinian Colonies were established, and pioneers from all parts of the world settled in the Holy Land. We must turn to our history books for a full account of the events which followed—the inspiring leadership of Herzl, the Balfour Declaration of 1917, the constant struggle to bring persecuted Jews to their Homeland and the strife between Arab and Jew. The climax was reached when Great Britain announced to the United Nations that, on May 15th, 1948, she would surrender the Mandate over Palestine which had been entrusted to her by the League of Nations in 1922. The *Va'ad Leumi* (People's Council) met immediately and announced to the world the formation of a provisional government.

On Friday the 5th of *Iyyar*, 5708, corresponding to the 14th of May, 1948, the newly elected Prime Minister, David Ben-Gurion, read the Jewish Declaration of Independence and announced: 'We hereby proclaim the establishment of the Jewish State in Palestine to be called Israel.' The severest test was to come: on the very next day the armies of seven Arab States began to attack Israel. The heroism of Israel's troops and of all her people, throughout the successful Battle for Freedom, recalled the courage of the ancient Maccabees. The new State of Israel was, in 1949, elected the fifty-ninth member of the United Nations.

Although the 5th of *Iyyar* occurs during *Sephirah* (the *Omer* period), the Chief Rabbinate of Israel permits celebrations on the anniversary of Independence Day, and has drawn up a special *Tikkun* containing an Order of Service, in which sections of the *Hallel* are included. In other countries, too, the day is marked by Services of Prayer and Thanksgiving to commemorate a great event in Jewish history which we have been privileged to witness in our own days.

CHAPTER 12

DAYS OF SORROW

1 The Four Fasts

In memory of happenings connected with the destruction of the Temple, four fasts are kept. They are mentioned by the prophet Zechariah (viii, 19) as *the fast of the fourth month and the fast of the fifth, the fast of the seventh and the fast of the tenth.* The four fasts are:

(i) The 10th of *Teveth*—עֲשָׂרָה בְּטֵבֵת: On this day the siege of Jerusalem by Nebuchadnezzar began. In *Israel* it is also observed as a Day of Memorial for the six million Jews who suffered martyrs' deaths during the Nazi terror in the second world war, 1939-1945.

(ii) The 17th of *Tammuz*—שִׁבְעָה עָשָׂר בְּתַמּוּז: In the time of the First Temple the walls of Jerusalem were breached on the 9th of *Tammuz* (II Kings xxv, 3 and 4); in the case of the Second Temple the 17th of *Tammuz* was the day the walls of the Capital were breached by the Romans, and that day was selected to be observed as the fast. Also on the 17th of *Tammuz*, records the Mishnah *Taanith* (iv, 6), four other disasters befell our forefathers: Moses, in anger, broke the tables of stone, on which the Ten Commandments were written, when he saw the Israelites worshipping the golden calf; the continual burnt offerings ceased during the siege of Jerusalem, because of the dearth of cattle; and Apostomos, a Syrian officer, burnt the scrolls of the Torah and set up an idol in the Sanctuary.

(iii) The 9th of *Av*—תִּשְׁעָה בְּאָב : This was the day on which the First Temple was destroyed by Nebuchadnezzar in 586 B.C.E. and the Second Temple by Titus in 70 C.E.

On this day also, states the Mishnah, God decreed that the older generation of Israelites should not enter the Land of Israel (Num. xiv, 28 ff); Bethar was captured (in 135 C.E.); and Jerusalem was ploughed up by command of Hadrian.

(iv) The 3rd of *Tishri*: Gedaliah, who had been appointed by Nebuchadnezzar as Governor of the Jews left in Palestine, was assassinated on the third of *Tishri*; and much suffering followed for the Jewish people. The fast is known as צוֹם גְּדַלְיָה—the fast of Gedaliah.

With the exception of *Tishah B'Av*, the fasting on all these days, as well as on *Taanith Esther* (see p. 89), begins at daybreak and lasts until nightfall, but we are allowed to carry out our daily occupations. In the Synagogue, both in the *Shacharith* and *Minchah* Services, a special reading from the Torah (Ex. xxxii, 11-14; xxxiv, 1-10) tells how Moses interceded with God on the people's behalf after the incident of the golden calf. The afternoon's *Haphtarah* is from Isaiah (lv, 6-lvi, 8) in which the prophet calls on the people to repent.

When these fasts fall on a Sabbath one of them, the Fast of Esther, is observed on the previous Thursday, but all the others, including *Tishah B'Av*, are kept on the next day, Sunday, and the fast is then known as נִדְחֶה— 'postponed' fast.

The three weeks between the 17th of *Tammuz* and *Tishah B'Av* are kept as a period of mourning. No joyous occasions, such as marriages, are arranged. The three

Haphtaroth read on the Sabbaths during these weeks are called ג' דְּפוּרְעָנוּתָא—i.e. the three (*Haphtaroth*) of rebuke. The first two are taken from the Book of Jeremiah (i, 1-ii, 3) and ii, 4-28; iii, 4) and the third from Isaiah (i, 1-27). The prophetic messages rebuke the people for their sins.

2 The 9th of Av

This fast, like *Yom Kippur*, is observed for a complete day: it begins at sunset on the eighth day of *Av* and ends at nightfall on the ninth. If it is at all possible, we refrain from our normal tasks at least until midday.

As a sign of mourning we eat no meat and drink no wine from the 1st of *Av* until noon on the 10th: our Rabbis tell us that the fire which destroyed the Temple continued burning throughout the tenth day of the month. The only exceptions are the Sabbath and, with certain reservations, a *Seudath Mitzvah* (see p. 62).

The Synagogue Services: In the Synagogue, on *Tishah B'Av*, there is an atmosphere of mourning. The Ark Curtain and other coverings are removed; congregants take off their shoes and sit on low chairs. During *Shacharith*, the *Tephillin* and *Tallith* are not worn but are put on at the *Minchah* Service. At the *Maariv* and *Shacharith* Services, a number of elegies known as קִינוֹת are recited. Composed by Jewish poets in the Middle Ages they record many sad events in Jewish history apart from the Destruction of the Temples. For instance, they tell of the martyrdom of the ten Rabbis, among them R. Akiba, who were put to death by the Romans, and of the massacre of German Jews during the first and second Crusades. The composers include Solomon Gabirol (eleventh century) and Judah Halevi (twelfth century) of Spain. In Halevi's Elegies of Zion, which form the last section of the *Kinoth*, the poet's love and yearning for the Holy Land are expressed in language of great beauty. At the Evening Service, the Book of Lamentations—אֵיכָה (see p. 27) is read.

The Torah reading at the *Shacharith* Service is taken from Deut. iv, 25-40 and deals with God's forgiveness of penitents; the *Haphtarah* (Jer. viii, 13 - ix, 23) foretells the punishment which will overtake the Kingdom of Judah. The Torah and *Haphtarah* readings at the *Minchah* Service are the same as on the other fast days.

During the seven weeks between *Tishah B'Av* and *Rosh Hashanah*, the *Haphtaroth* read on the Sabbath are taken from Isaiah. They contain comforting messages known as דְּנֶחֱמָתָא ז'—i.e. the seven (*Haphtaroth*) of consolation (see p. 102).

שֵׁנִי חֲמִישִׁי וְשֵׁנִי 3 lit., second, fifth and second (days of the week).

During the months of *Iyyar* and *Marcheshvan* these three days are kept voluntarily by some as fast days, to atone for any sins they may have committed on the preceding *Pesach* and *Succoth*. The practice is based on Job's bringing of special sacrifices after festive occasions (Job. i). In some communities, in England for instance, these fasts are kept on the Monday, Thursday and following Monday immediately preceding *Lag Ba'Omer* (the 18th of *Iyyar*) and *Rosh Chodesh Kislev* respectively; but in America and some other countries, the first Monday, Thursday and following Monday of *Iyyar* and *Marcheshvan* are the fast days.

The days were chosen as appropriate ones on which to pray for forgiveness, because, according to our Rabbis, Moses ascended Mount Sinai to receive the Second Tablets on a Thursday, and descended on a Monday.

4 Yom Kippur Katan

The day before *Rosh Chodesh* is observed by some as a fast day. It is known as יוֹם כִּפּוּר קָטָן, i.e. the minor *Yom Kippur*. When *Rosh Chodesh* falls on a Sabbath or Sunday, the fast is observed on the preceding Thursday.

CHAPTER 13

SOME IMPORTANT SABBATHS

1 Four Special Sabbaths 2 Other Important Sabbaths – *Shabbath Hagadol* – *Shabbath Shuvah* – *Shabbath Chazon* – *Shabbath Nachamu* – *Shabbath Rosh Chodesh* – *Shabbath Mevorechim* – *Shabbath Bereshith* – *Shabbath Shirah*

1 **Four Special Sabbaths**

Four Sabbaths of special religious and historical significance are classed together in the Mishnah (*Megillah* iii, 4). On each of them, a portion of the Law is read in Synagogue from a second *Sepher Torah*, accompanied by an appropriate *Haphtarah*. These Sabbaths occur between the end of *Shevat* and the first of *Nisan*. They are:

(i) שַׁבָּת שְׁקָלִים—'The Sabbath relating to the Shekels': The Torah reading, taken from Exodus xxx, 11-16, contains the law commanding males over the age of twenty to contribute half a shekel yearly towards the upkeep of the Tabernacle, *to make atonement for their souls*. The *Haphtarah* (II Kings xii, 1-17) describes how, in the reign of King Joash, the people brought money for repairing the breaches in the Temple. These contributions were paid, in Temple times, by the first of *Nisan*, from which date the year for purchasing public sacrifices began. A month's notice was given by the *Beth Din* on the first of *Adar*, and messengers went through the Land of Israel and the Diaspora to remind people that the money was due.

These Biblical passages are read on the Sabbath before the first of *Adar*, or on the day itself when it falls on a Sabbath—hence the name *Shabbath Shekalim*. Besides

99

being historically interesting, they remind us of our duties towards the upkeep of the Synagogue and other worthy communal causes.

(ii) שַׁבָּת זָכוֹר—'The Sabbath relating to "Remember"' (i.e. the section from Deut. xxv, 17-19, beginning with the words *Remember* (*what Amalek did to you on the way when you came out of Egypt*): Amalek, who launched an unjustified attack on the people of Israel during their march through the wilderness ('*for he had no fear of God*') was heavily defeated by Joshua's army. In the *Haphtarah* (1 Samuel xv, 2-34) the extermination of the wicked Amalekites by Saul and his army is described. These passages are read on the Sabbath before *Purim*, because Haman the Agagite was, according to tradition, directly descended from Agag, king of the Amalekites.

(iii) שַׁבָּת פָּרָה—'The Sabbath relating to the (Red) Heifer': We read, on this Sabbath (from Numbers xix, 1-22) about the sacrifice of the Red Heifer and the ceremony of purification. The ashes of the Red Heifer were, after certain rites, sprinkled on the third and seventh day over a person who had become defiled through contact with the dead. In the *Haphtarah* (Ezekiel xxxvi, 16-38), the prophet beseeches the exiled people of Israel to cleanse themselves from their sins and be prepared for the time when the Holy Land will be restored.

In Temple times, every male Israelite was expected to come to Jerusalem to offer the sacrificial Paschal Lamb on the 14th of *Nisan*, but he could not do so if he was unclean. So these passages are read before Passover—on the first Sabbath after *Purim*, or on the second Sabbath after *Purim*, when the 15th or 16th of *Adar* falls on a Saturday. They remind us of the importance of physical and moral purity.

(iv) שַׁבָּת הַחֹדֶשׁ—'The Sabbath relating to THE month (of *Nisan*)' (i.e. the section from Ex. xii, 1-20, beginning *This month* (*shall be unto you the beginning of the months*), which deals with the laws of the Passover). The *Haphtarah* (Ezekiel xlv, 16-xlvi, 18) describes the sacrifices, including those of Passover, to be offered up in the Temple conceived by Ezekiel in his vision. These passages are read in the Synagogue on the Sabbath before the first of *Nisan* or on the day itself if it be a Sabbath. They recall to mind the everlasting lesson of the deliverance from Egypt and the blessings of freedom.

2 Other Important Sabbaths

Apart from the four Sabbaths already described, there are a number of other specially named Sabbaths. They are:

(i) שַׁבָּת הַגָּדוֹל—'*The Great Sabbath*': This is the Sabbath before Passover, and the following are three of the reasons which have been given for its title—

(*a*) The tenth of *Nisan*, when the call came to the Israelites to choose a lamb for a sacrifice, fell, it is said, on a Sabbath. Such an offering would have been abominable to the Egyptians (see Ex. viii, 26), yet they did not interfere in any way. So it was a great and miraculous day for our people.

(*b*) Some scholars suggest that the Sabbath before all important Festivals was called a 'Great' Sabbath, when the people were taught about the observances of the coming Holy Day. In time, the name became associated only with the Sabbath before Passover.

(*c*) In the *Haphtarah* (Malachi iii, 4-24), describing the forthcoming day of God's Judgment, the prophet announces, in the name of God, *Behold I will send you Elijah, the prophet, before the great and terrible day of the Lord.*

(ii) שַׁבָּת שׁוּבָה—'*The Sabbath of Repentance*' (i.e. the Sabbath between *Rosh Hashanah* and *Yom Kippur*) (see p. 82).

(iii) שַׁבָּת חֲזוֹן—'*The Sabbath of the Vision*' (of Isaiah): This is the Sabbath before *Tishah B'Av*, and is so called because the *Haphtarah* (Isaiah i) begins with the words '*the vision (of Isaiah)*'. In his message, the prophet rebukes the people for being unfaithful to God.

(iv) שַׁבָּת נַחֲמוּ—'*The Sabbath of Comfort*': On this Sabbath, which is the one that comes after the 9th of *Av*, the first of the seven *Haphtaroth* of Comfort (see p. 97) is read. The *Haphtarah* (Isaiah xl) begins with the words 'Comfort ye, (my people).' The prophet foretells that Israel will be restored to its land.

(v) שַׁבָּת רֹאשׁ חֹדֶשׁ—'*The Sabbath on which Rosh Chodesh falls*': Two scrolls are taken from the Ark. From the first, the weekly *Sidra* is read; and from the second, a special portion, Num. xxviii, 9-15. It deals with the sacrifices offered on the Sabbath and New Moon. In the *Haphtarah* (Isaiah lxvi) the prophet speaks words of comfort to those who are faithful to God in spite of the ridicule of their enemies. The day will come when, *from one new moon to another, and from one Sabbath to another, all flesh shall come to worship before Me, saith the Lord.*

When *Rosh Chodesh* falls on a Sunday, a special *Haphtarah* (I Samuel xx, 18-42) is read on the previous day (Sabbath). It is known as מָחָר חֹדֶשׁ—'tomorrow is the New Moon'—because the opening incident occurs on the eve of *Rosh Chodesh*; '*Then Jonathan said to him (David) Tomorrow is the new moon.*' Jonathan undertakes to sound his father, Saul, on his attitude towards David.

On the following three Sabbaths no special *Haphtarah* is read:

(vi) שַׁבָּת מְבָרְכִים—'*The Sabbath on which we Pray for the Blessing (of the New Moon)*': This is the Sabbath before any *Rosh Chodesh*. The *Yehi Ratzon* prayer is recited. We ask God 'to renew unto us this coming month for good and for blessing.'

(vii) שַׁבָּת בְּרֵאשִׁית—'*The Sabbath of Bereshith*': The first Sabbath after *Succoth*. We start the first *Sidra*, once again, in the Reading of the Torah.

(viii) שַׁבָּת שִׁירָה—'*The Sabbath when the Song*' (of Moses) is read from the Torah (*Parashath Beshallach*). He sang it after the crossing of the Red Sea (Ex. xv, 1-18).

CHAPTER 14

THE DIETARY LAWS

1 The Purpose of the Dietary Laws 2 Some Basic Laws
3 *Shechitah* 4 Meat and Milk 5 Vegetable Food

1 The Purpose of the Dietary Laws

Laws on the food we may or may not eat are given in a
number of passages in the Torah. The reason for their
observance, given again and again, is put (in Leviticus xi,
44) in these words: *For I am the Lord your God; sanctify
yourselves therefore and be holy, for I am holy*. The Torah
thus clearly states that the purpose of the dietary laws is
to attain the ideal of holiness. Israel, a people consecrated
to God, must strive to be holy by following His ways and
keeping His commandments, and by not doing those
things which the Torah calls impure and abominable.

This needs great self-control. It is invaluable in
training us to resist temptations which would lead us
away from righteous paths. In addition, the Dietary Laws,
like many other commandments, distinguish us from other
peoples and prevent us from assimilating with them. So
they have been vital in preserving the identity and purity
of the Jewish race.

The benefits for the Jewish people of strict adherence
to the Dietary Laws have been discussed by many writers.
Maimonides, in his 'Guide to the Perplexed,' suggests
that the object of the laws is to restrain the growth of
desire and the idea that eating and drinking are man's
sole aim. A number of writers point out that some of the
forbidden foods are injurious to health. Others, taking

the humane approach, show that many of the laws of *Shechitah* (mentioned later in this chapter) are designed to spare the animal as much pain as possible.

These reasons are sound, but they must be considered as supplementary to the chief aim mentioned in the Torah —to attain the state of holiness.

2 Some Basic Laws

The basic laws relating to food come under two headings:

(i) food which is *kasher*—כָּשֵׁר (i.e. 'fit' to be eaten in accordance with Jewish law) and

(ii) food which is *terefah*—טְרֵפָה (this word, meaning 'torn,' originally referred to animals mauled by a wild beast, but is now applied to any kind of food forbidden by Jewish law).

(*a*) Only cattle or beasts with the following character-istics may be eaten: (1) a divided hoof which must be wholly cloven-footed, i.e. the hoof must be com-pletely cloven or split; and (2) the animal must chew the cud, i.e. must bring back the food from the stomach into its mouth, chewing it at leisure (Lev. xi, 3). Such animals are known as 'clean' cattle or 'clean' beasts— חַיָּה טְהוֹרָה or בְּהֵמָה טְהוֹרָה. The list of permitted animals, which includes the ox, sheep and goat, is given in Deut. xiv, 4 and 5. Examples of 'unclean' animals—בְּהֵמָה טְמֵאָה—are given in verse 7 of the same chapter and include the camel, hare and pig.

(*b*) The signs of clean and unclean birds are not stated in the Torah but are mentioned in the Talmud. Examples of unclean birds, among them birds of prey, are to be found in Lev. xi, 13-19. We are allowed to eat only birds that are traditionally known to be 'clean' such as the hen, goose or turkey.

(c) We are told in Lev. xi, 9, that only fish having both fins and scales are permitted as food. Eels, as well as sea animals such as seals and whales, are forbidden.

(d) Insects must not be eaten. Although four kinds of locusts are permitted, we do not know the exact type to which the Torah refers (Lev. xi, 22). So the Rabbinic authorities forbade every kind of locust.

(e) *Every creeping thing which creeps upon the earth shall be an abomination* (Lev. xi, 41). Included in this prohibition are crabs, lobsters and shell fish such as snails and oysters.

(f) The milk of unclean animals and the eggs of unclean birds are forbidden. The oil and roe of unclean fish such as caviare, which is prepared from the roe of the sturgeon, may not be eaten. Bee's honey is allowed as the Rabbis considered that honey does not contain any part of the insect. It was regarded as the juice of the flower sucked by the bee and later discharged.

(g) Those parts of the fat of all clean animals burnt on the altar when sacrifices were offered, i.e. the fat covering the stomach and the kidneys (Lev. iii, 3, 4), are forbidden as food (Lev. vii, 23). Such fat is called חֵלֶב and must be removed by the process known as porging. Fat permitted as food is called שׁוּמָן.

(h) When Jacob and the Angel wrestled, the Angel *touched the hollow of Jacob's thigh in the sinew of the hip* (Gen. xxxii, 33), and for this reason, the Bible tells us, the Children of Israel do not eat the sinew of an animal's hip. The גִּיד הַנָּשֶׁה—sinew of the hip—must be removed from the hind-quarters of cattle before they can be eaten.

(i) Eating the blood of beasts and birds is not allowed, *for the life of all flesh is the blood thereof* (Lev. xvii, 14). To make sure that the blood is removed and the meat made *kasher*, we carry out this process: after the meat has been soaked in water for thirty minutes, it is placed on a slanting draining board so that the blood may flow more easily; then the meat is covered on all sides with salt which, after an hour, is removed by rinsing. Eggs found inside poultry, even in their shells, must be salted separately in the same way as meat. If a speck of blood is found in an egg, it may not be eaten.

(*j*) An animal and its young must not be slaughtered on the same day (Lev. xxii, 28). As Maimonides explains, this commandment was given to prevent cruelty, for even among animals the mother has tender feelings for its young.

(*k*) For a similar reason, it is forbidden to cut off a piece of flesh from a living animal – אֵבֶר מִן הַחַי – for our food.

3 **Shechitah:** שְׁחִיטָה (method of 'slaughtering')

The commands on slaughtering clean animals and birds form part of the Oral Law, but they are referred to in the Written Law in Deut. xii, 21, 'You shall kill of your herd and of your flock which the Lord has given you, *as I have commanded you.*' It is impossible here to give a detailed account of the numerous regulations. One of the chief objects of *shechitah* is to spare the animal unnecessary pain, and the effectiveness of Jewish methods has been acknowledged by many leading non-Jewish authorities. *Shechitah* must be performed only by a skilled and pious person called a *Shochet*—שׁוֹחֵט—who knows the laws thoroughly and has been examined by a Rabbinic authority such as a *Beth Din*. The knife he uses must be very sharp and free from any notches which might tear the flesh. After reciting a special blessing he must carry out his task quickly and accurately to produce instant unconsciousness through the rapid discharge of blood.

If any part of the carcase is found to be diseased, it is declared *terefah* and may not be eaten.

4 Meat and Milk: בָּשָׂר בְּחָלָב

You shall not seethe a kid in its mother's milk. This law, repeated three times in the Torah (Ex. xxiii, 19 and xxxiv, 26 and Deut. xiv, 21), is explained by the Rabbis to indicate three prohibitions: (*a*) meat and milk may not be boiled together; (*b*) meat and milk may not be eaten together; and (*c*) no benefit may be derived from such a mixture. Therefore, every Jewish household should have two sets of pots and pans, crockery, cutlery etc.—one for meat dishes and the other for milk. After meat has been eaten an interval of between three to six hours—according to the custom of the community—is required before milk food may be eaten.

5 Vegetable Food

There are some commandments about vegetable products and fruits, which, although connected with the soil of *Eretz Yisrael*, must nevertheless be observed by Jews in every country (see *Kiddushin* i, 9).

(i) The fruit of trees which grows during the first three years after planting is called עָרְלָה—'uncircumcised'— and is forbidden (Lev. xix, 23). In Temple times the fruit of the fourth year was either consumed in Jerusalem or redeemed for money which was spent in Jerusalem on food.

(ii) The new corn of each yearly crop, known as חָדָשׁ— 'new'—can be eaten only after the second day of *Pesach*, when, in Temple times, the *Omer* was brought as a wave-offering (Lev. xxiii, 10-14).

(iii) The grafting of trees and sowing a vineyard with two different kinds of seeds is forbidden. This prohibition comes in the category of כִּלְאַיִם—lit. 'the junction of two' or the intermingling of two different species (Deut. xxii, 9).

(The wearing of 'a mingled stuff,' i.e. of wool and linen, called שַׁעַטְנֵז, is also forbidden. See Deut. xxii, 11).

Mention should be made of the law relating to חַלָּה the portion of dough given to the priests in Temple times: *When you eat of the bread of the land, you shall set apart a portion for a gift to the Lord. Of the first of your dough, you shall set apart a cake for a gift* (Numbers xv, 19 and 20). Nowadays, as we cannot carry out this commandment, a small piece of the dough used by ourselves or the Jewish baker, when preparing bread, is separated and burned. A special blessing is recited.

CHAPTER 15

THE OUTWARD SIGNS

1 The *Tephillin* 2 The *Mezuzah* 3 The *Tzitzith*

So immersed are we in everyday tasks that we are apt to forget the high principles which should guide us. The Torah has provided a number of visible signs which remind us of our duties. Three mentioned in the *Shema* are: the *Tephillin, Mezuzah* and *Tzitzith*.

1 **The Tephillin:** תְּפִלִּין

The word is, perhaps, the plural Aramaic form of *Tephillah*, i.e. prayer. *And you shall bind them for a sign upon your hand and they shall be for frontlets between your eyes* — this commandment, in the *Shema* (Deut. vi, 8 and xi, 18), is also repeated in two other Biblical passages with slight variations (Ex. xiii, 9 and 16).

The four sections containing these verses are:

(i) Ex. xiii, 1-10, on the Laws relating to the dedication of male first-borns to the service of God and the sacrifice of the male firstlings of animals. Israelites are reminded for all time that they were spared the disaster which came to Egyptian first-borns before the Exodus.

(ii) Ex. xiii, 11-16, repeating the Law of the first-born and charging the father (in answering his son's question about the meaning of the commandment) to describe the epic deliverance from Egypt.

(iii) Deut. vi, 4-9, the first paragraph of the *Shema*, on the Unity of God etc. (see p. 43).

(iv) Deut. xi, 13-21, the second paragraph of the *Shema*, on reward and punishment (see p. 43).

These four sections which stress the Divine Rule of the Universe, the Unity of God and the Redemption from Egypt—three important teachings of the Jewish faith— are written down by a scribe on parchment, and this is enclosed in a case known as בַּיִת—'a house,' i.e. container. In the תְּפִלָּה שֶׁל יָד worn on the left hand, all are written on one piece of parchment, whereas in the תְּפִלָּה שֶׁל ראֹשׁ worn on the head, the sections are written on separate pieces of parchment and placed in four different compartments. Each of the leather straps attached to the *Tephillin* is called a רְצוּעָה. The blessing for the *tephillah shel yad* ends with the words, 'to lay *tephillin*,' and that for the *tephillah shel rosh* with the words, 'concerning the command of *tephillin*.'

Most *Siddurim* print a meditation to be recited before laying the *Tephillin*, setting out their purpose: 'He has commanded us to lay the *Tephillin* on the hand as a memorial of His outstretched arm; and opposite the heart so that we can subject the longings and designs of our heart to His service; and upon the head over against the brain, teaching us that the mind, together with all our senses and faculties, must be subjected to His service.'

The duty of laying *Tephillin* falls upon every male over the age of thirteen, when he must fulfil all the religious precepts (see p. 115). *Tephillin* are not worn on a Sabbath or festival day as these themselves are signs of God's covenant with Israel (see p. 55).

2 The Mezuzah: מְזוּזָה

And you shall write them upon the doorposts of your house and upon your gates (Deut. vi, 9.) We keep this command by fixing the *mezuzah* on the doors of our houses and living-rooms. It is placed on the right-hand post (about a third of the way down) in a slanting position, so that the upper part inclines towards the house or room. The *mezuzah* is a piece of parchment on which a scribe has written the first two paragraphs of the *Shema* and which is placed in a case with the word שַׁדַּי—Almighty—on the back.

The *mezuzah* reminds of God's presence and protection, and of our duty to obey His commandments.

3 The Tzitzith: צִיצִית

And it shall be unto you for a fringe that you look on it and remember all the commandments of the Lord and do them (Num. xv, 39). The third paragraph of the *Shema* clearly states that the *Tzitzith* serve to remind us to *observe* the Divine precepts. During the whole day every male must wear beneath his outer garments, the אַרְבַּע כַּנְפוֹת—lit. 'the four corners' of the garments (see Deut. xxii, 12), or, as it is sometimes called, the טַלִּית קָטָן—'the smaller *Tallith*.' Before putting it on, he says a blessing ending with the words 'concerning the command of *Tzitzith*.' In early times the *Tallith* was a mantle worn as an outer garment, with fringes at the four corners. By the thirteenth century, as Jews associated more and more with non-Jewish neighbours, the practice of wearing the *Tallith Katan* had grown. The larger *Tallith* is worn in Synagogue during Morning Services, but on *Yom Kippur* it is worn throughout the day and on *Tishah B'Av* at *Minchah* instead of in the morning (see p. 96). The blessing concludes with the words 'to enwrap ourselves with the *Tzitzith*'.

It was once possible to fulfill the command of having 'a thread of blue' in the fringe. The colour came from a special dye obtained from a rare shell-fish known as *chilazon*. The Talmud tells us that this fish could not be identified and so the exact ingredients of the dye were unknown. For this reason we have white threads only on our *Tzitzith* today.

THROUGHOUT OUR LIVES

To mark various important occasions in our lives, special ceremonies are performed. This chapter deals briefly with some of them.

1 בְּרִית מִילָה—The Covenant of Circumcision

This is also known as the Covenant of Abraham to whom God said, *This is My covenant which you shall keep between Me and you, and your seed after you; every male among you shall be circumcised ... he that is eight days old* (Gen. xvii, 10-12). The ceremony is observed on the eighth day, even if it falls on the Sabbath and *Yom Kippur*, and can be postponed only on medical advice. The *Mohel*—מוֹהֵל—who performs the operation is a specialist who has passed a searching examination by Rabbinic authorities and has been granted a certificate of qualification.

The boy is first placed on a cushion on a chair, called 'the chair of Elijah'- Rabbinical tradition has it that in recognition of Elijah's religious zeal it was ordained in Israel that no *brith milah* would be celebrated except in his presence. The child is transferred to the lap of the person who is to hold it during the ceremony and who is called the בַּעַל בְּרִית—lit. 'the person holding (the child to be brought into) the covenant,' or the *sandek*, a Greek word meaning 'godfather.' Immediately after the operation, a Hebrew name is given to the child.

114

This covenant between Israel and God is yet another test of our loyalty towards Him, and has been cherished by the Jewish people throughout their history.

A girl is given her Hebrew name generally on the Sabbath after birth, when the father is called up to the Reading of the Law in Synagogue and a special prayer is recited.

2 Redemption of the First-born: פִּדְיוֹן הַבֵּן

The Torah states that every male first-born was to be consecrated to the service of God, recalling the miraculous deliverance in Egypt (Ex. xiii, 13). Eventually, the tribe of Levi was chosen to supply the priests and servants of the Sanctuary, *instead of all the first-born . . . among the children of Israel* (Num. iii, 12). The first-born was accordingly redeemed, to free him from this obligation, *from a month old . . . for five shekels of silver* (Num. xviii, 16).

The redemption ceremony is held on the thirty-first day after birth, but is postponed until the following day if the thirty-first day be a Sabbath or *Yomtov*. Five shekels or its equivalent in silver, is the amount of the redemption money which the father hands to a *Cohen*. Should the father be a *Cohen* or a *Levite*, or the mother be the daughter of a *Cohen* or *Levite*, they are exempt from the obligation of Redemption. The complete Service can be found in the *Siddur*.

3 Barmitzvah: בַּר מִצְוָה (lit. 'Son of the Commandment')

This term is applied to the boy who has reached the age of thirteen years and a day—when, in accordance with Jewish Law, he becomes personally responsible for carrying out the Commandments. 'At thirteen,' says Judah ben Tema, 'the age is reached for the fulfilment of the

Commandments,' (Avoth v, 24). Although in the Talmud the term *Barmitzvah* is applied to every adult Jew, there is sufficient evidence to show that the event was marked in early times by a special ceremony. The increased significance of the occasion is a much later development, dating from about 600 years ago. A month before he is Barmitzvah the boy begins training to lay *Tephillin*. On the Sabbath following his thirteenth birthday, he is called up to the Reading of the Law and may recite a part or the whole of the *Sidra*, and the *Haphtarah*.

4 Marriage

The Jewish concept of marriage is an act of קִדּוּשִׁין—sanctification, to be regarded as a Divine institution. This is the basis of the many laws enacted by the Rabbis to uphold the dignity of man and woman. At one time there were two distinct ceremonies of betrothal and marriage. The betrothal was a solemn bond, binding the couple to be married within a fixed period. Nowadays, the betrothal and marriage are combined.

The wedding ceremony takes place under a חֻפָּה—Canopy—symbolizing the home the couple are to set up. The bridegroom solemnly declares 'Behold you are consecrated to me by this ring according to the Law of Moses and of Israel.' The כְּתֻבָּה—'written' Marriage Contract—is read. It is in Aramaic and states the obligations of the bridegroom to his bride. The contents of the concluding שֶׁבַע בְּרָכוֹת—Seven Benedictions (quoted in the *Talmud*)—are: (i) the blessing over wine; (ii) praise of God who created the Universe; (iii) and who created man; (iv) and who created man in His own image and created woman; (v) a prayer for the restoration of Zion; (vi) for the happiness of bride and bridegroom; (vii) praise of God who created the joys of man and wife, love, brotherhood and peace.

Finally the bridegroom breaks a glass, recalling—it is suggested—the destruction of the Temple and reminding us to temper joy with solemnity.

5 חֲנֻכַּת הַבַּיִת—Consecration of a House

The dedication of the altar and Temple in ancient times may well be the basis of our custom to hold a special Service of Consecration when we acquire a new house. After the recital of appropriate psalms, four sections of the long alphabetical psalm (cxix) are said, forming the Hebrew word *Berachah*. In this way we ask God to bless and protect our homes where 'we will meditate on His precepts and look towards His paths' (Ps. cxix, 15).

6 Death and Mourning

Death is as natural as birth. Our souls return to God and, we believe, enjoy the blessings of the World to Come—עוֹלָם הַבָּא. Our Rabbis warn us not to speculate about life after death, but rather to concentrate on life in this world—עוֹלָם הַזֶּה and faithfully carry out the laws of God which have been revealed to us.

Before burying a near relative, i.e. parent, child, brother or sister, the mourners tear part of their clothes as a symbol of grief. They recite the benediction 'Blessed art thou, etc., the true Judge,'—acknowledging, in this way justice of God's decree—צִדּוּק הַדִּין. Before and on the day of burial, the Hebrew term for mourners is אוֹנְנִים. Afterwards they are called אֲבֵלִים. Mourning is observed for seven days—שִׁבְעָה—during which the mourners stay at home (except on the Sabbath), wear no shoes and sit on low stools. At services held in the house, *Kaddish* is recited. Children continue to mourn a parent for twelve months; other relatives mourn for thirty days—שְׁלֹשִׁים. During these periods mourners take no part in festivities.

Respect for loved ones who have died must continue throughout our lives. About a year after the death a tombstone—מַצֵּבָה—is consecrated, and on the actual anniversary (*Yahrzeit*, a German word meaning 'anniversary'), a light is kindled, symbolizing the soul of the departed, and *Kaddish* is recited in Synagogue.

A memorial prayer known as יִזְכֹּר, from the opening word '(May God) remember (the soul etc)', is said in Synagogue on *Yom Kippur*, the last day of *Pesach*, the second day of *Shavuoth*, and on *Shemini Atzereth*.

More important than these customs is our resolve to be faithful to the teaching of our parents 'whose desire it was'—in the words of the Memorial Prayer—'to train us in the good and righteous way, to teach us Thy statutes and commandments, and to instruct us to do justice and to love mercy.'

CHAPTER 17

BETWEEN MAN AND GOD

1 The Fear of God **2** The Love of God **3** *Chillul Hashem* and
Kiddush Hashem **4** The Divine Example

Many fundamental Jewish beliefs and practices have
been presented in this book. Now it will turn to some
of the ethical and moral teachings of Judaism; in other
words, to ideal principles of human conduct and character,
according to Judaism. In illustration there will be quotations from the Bible and Rabbinic literature (the biblical
quotations being in italics).

Obedience to the Divine precepts, we have seen,
enables man to reach the aim of holiness set by the
Creator and to lead an upright life. Sincere prayer and
repentance help us to express our innermost feelings and
establish a personal relationship with our Father in
Heaven. By our moral conduct we show our reverence
and love for, and loyalty towards, God.

1 יִרְאַת ה׳—**The Fear of God, or** יִרְאַת שָׁמַיִם—**the Fear of Heaven**

This does not imply that we must be afraid of God in
the sense that we fear His punishment for our misdeeds.
It rather expresses our awe at being in the presence of the
King of the Universe, who demands perfection from those
He has created, and who rewards the righteous and
punishes the wicked. Remembering this, we shall commit
no wrong by actions, words or thoughts that displease
Him. It is a fear which leads to love, for it recognizes that

the Divine purpose of creation is to provide happiness and peace for all mankind.

And now, Israel, what does the Lord your God require of you, but to fear the Lord your God, to walk in all His ways, and to love Him, and to serve the Lord your God with all your heart and with all your soul (Deut. x, 12).

Happy is the man who fears the Lord, who delights greatly in His Commandments (Ps. cxii, 1, 2).

Rava bar Rav Huna said, 'A person who is possessed of learning but not of the fear of Heaven can be compared to a treasurer to whom the keys of the inner doors have been handed but not those of the outer doors (and therefore cannot complete his task)' (*Shabbath* 31a).

2 אַהֲבַת הַשֵׁם—**The Love of God** (lit., Love of the Name)

Wherever the Bible mentions the love of God there follows a command to keep His precepts. We can prove our love of God by obeying His Law without thought of reward and in spite of sacrifices we may have to make. This was the example set by Abraham, our forefather, who was put to the test by being asked to offer up his dearest possession, his son Isaac. Appropriately, he is named by God, through the mouth of Isaiah the prophet, '*Abraham, who showed love for Me*' (Isaiah xli, 8). Such complete surrender of the heart and mind to God's Will is expressed by the Rabbis as קַבָּלַת עוֹל מַלְכוּת שָׁמַיִם— accepting for oneself the yoke of the Kingdom of Heaven.

You shall love the Lord your God with all your heart and with all your soul and with all your might (Deut. vi, 5).

To love the Lord your God, to hearken to His voice, and to cleave to Him (Deut. xxx, 20). Our Rabbis comment: 'A man should not say "I shall study the Bible so that people should call me learned, or I shall study the Mishnah that they call me Rabbi" . . . but learn out of love and honour will come in the end' (*Nedarim* 62a).

Judah ben Tema said, 'Be as strong as a leopard, light as an eagle, fleet as a hart, and strong as a lion, to do the will of your Father who is in heaven' (*Avoth*, v, 23).

3 חִלּוּל הַשֵּׁם—Profaning the Name of God

Every Jew bears the responsibility of guarding the honour of Judaism and not bringing disgrace on his people. If he commits an offence against the laws of the country he lives in, or against his neighbour, whether Jew or non-Jew, he is guilty of *Chillul Hashem*. The Third Commandment forbids us to 'take the name of the Lord in vain.' We must not utter His name frivolously or carelessly, whether in Hebrew or another language.

קִדּוּשׁ הַשֵּׁם—**Sanctifying the Name of God:** Conversely, our attitude must be positive: we must keep to God's ways, setting an example of uprightness to all mankind. On many a sad occasion has a cruel oppressor commanded Jews to disown the Divine laws against idolatry, immorality and murder. Our Rabbis decreed that on such occasions death is preferable to a transgression that would endanger the very existence of the Jewish nation. And thousands of Jewish martyrs have given up their lives for *Kiddush Hashem* rather than abandon their Faith.

And you shall not profane My holy name, but I will be sanctified among the Children of Israel (Lev. xxii, 32).

Neither repentance nor *Yom Kippur* nor suffering can atone for the man who has committed *Chillul Hashem* (*Yoma* 86a).

Rabbi Jochanan ben Berokah said, 'Whoever profanes the name of Heaven in secret will suffer the penalty in

public, whether he acts in ignorance or with intent'
(*Avoth* iv, 5).

You shall be holy, for I, the Lord your God am holy
(Lev. xix, 2).

4 The Divine Example

The source and inspiration of the righteous life, our
Rabbis tell us, are the Divine qualities of mercy enumer-
ated in Exodus xxxiv, 6 and 7. The thirteen Attributes—
שְׁלֹשׁ עֶשְׂרֵה מִדּוֹת—as they are called, were revealed by God
to Moses when he ascended Mount Sinai to receive the
second Tablets of Stone. *The Lord, the Lord, God, full of
compassion and gracious, slow to anger, abundant in goodness
and in truth, keeping mercy to the thousandth generation,
forgiving iniquity and transgression and sin, and will by no
means clear the guilty.* By following His example, man
co-operates with God in establishing a world based on
righteousness, mercy and love.

As the All-present is called merciful and gracious,
so should you be merciful and gracious and act
generously to all. As the Holy One, blessed be He, is
called righteous, so should you be righteous. As He
is called kindly in all His works, so should you be
kindly (*Sifre* Deut. para. 49).

You shall walk after the Lord your God (Deut. xiii, 5).
R. Chama ben Chanina said, 'This means that we
should follow the attributes of the Holy One, blessed be
He. As He clothed the naked (Adam and Eve) so
should you clothe the naked. As He visited the sick
(Abraham after his circumcision) so should you visit
the sick. As He comforted the mourners (Isaac after the
death of Abraham) so should you comfort the mourners.
As He buried the dead (Moses) so should you bury
the dead.' (*Sotah* 14a).

BETWEEN MAN AND MAN

Chapter nineteen of Leviticus contains many guiding principles for regulating everyday conduct. We are commanded to respect our parents, be kind to the poor, pay wages promptly to employees, deal honourably in business, not be a tale-bearer, love our neighbour, show friendship to the alien, and be just to both rich and poor. In many ways they correspond to the Ten Commandments. Significantly, we read at the very beginning of the chapter, *You shall be holy for I the Lord your God am holy.* The duty of carrying out these and all other righteous principles is an integral part of the Torah.

1 **Loyalty to the Community**

Man cannot live for himself alone. Every deed he performs, every word he utters, affects the life of his neighbour. To maintain a society based on the ideal of holiness man must co-operate with his neighbour. He must accept responsibility when he is asked to share in communal endeavour, support worthy causes, and uphold his people's good name. Nor must he do so for selfish reasons, but for 'the sake of Heaven.'

Hillel used to say, 'If I am not for myself, who is for me? Yet if I am for myself (only) what am I? And if not now, when?' (*Avoth* i, 14).

Hillel said, 'Separate not yourself from the community' (*Avoth* ii, 5).

All members of Israel are accountable for each other (*Shevuoth* 39a).

At a time when the community is living amidst trouble, a man should not say 'I shall go home and eat and drink. Peace be upon you, O my soul.' For if he does so Scripture says of him (Isaiah xxii, 14), *Surely this iniquity will not be atoned for by you until you die* (*Taanith* 11 a).

2 Loyalty to the State

Every Jew has the duty of loyalty to the Laws of the country he lives in unless it violates his religious beliefs and practices. An upright Jew is a good citizen, playing his part in all endeavours that make for the welfare of the State. He applies the teachings of Judaism on justice, righteousness and truth to his relations with his non-Jewish neighbour.

Seek the peace of the city whither I have caused you to be carried away captive, and pray unto the Lord for it; for in the peace thereof shall you have peace (Jer. xxix, 7).

Pray for the welfare of the Government, since but for the fear thereof men would swallow each other alive (*Avoth* iii, 2).

The law of the land is law (*Baba Kamma* 113a).

3 Brotherly Love

We must show love for our neighbour whatever his race, colour or creed, for we are all the children of one God and are equal in His sight. The people of Israel know what it means to be aliens in a foreign land, friendless, oppressed, and special compassion must be felt for those who have had to leave their own country. The Talmud mentions that the command to love or not to oppress the stranger occurs thirty-six times in the Torah.

You shall love your neighbour as yourself, I am the Lord (Lev. xix, 18).

The stranger who sojourns with you shall be to you as the home-born among you and you shall love him as yourself, for you were strangers in the Land of Egypt (Lev. xix, 34).

Have we not all one Father? Has not one God created us? (Malachi ii, 10).

And you shall love your neighbour as yourself. R. Akiba said 'This is the fundamental principle of the Torah' (*Sifra*).

Hillel was approached by a heathen who wished to be converted to Judaism on condition that he was taught the whole Torah while he stood on one foot. The Rabbi said to him 'What is hateful to yourself do not do to your fellowman. This is the whole of the Torah, the rest is its commentary. Go and study it' (*Shabbath* 31a).

Man was created as a single individual for the sake of the peace of mankind, so that a person should not say to his fellow 'My ancestor was greater than yours' (*Sanhedrin* iv, 5).

Who is the mightiest of all? He who turns his enemy into a friend (*Avoth d'R. Nathan* xxiii).

There are righteous individuals in all nations who will have a share in the World to Come (*Tosefta Sanhedrin* xiii, 2).

4 The Sanctity of Human Life

Life, given by God to man, is his most treasured possession. To destroy it wilfully is a transgression against God Himself. Physical force which endangers life or limb is equally a crime against the Creator; even to threaten violence brands the aggressor as wicked. Our duty is to save human life and not stand idly by when our fellow-man is in danger.

Thou shalt not murder (Ex. xx, 13).

Neither shall you stand idly by the blood of your neighbour (Lev. xix, 16).

He who destroys a human life is considered by Scripture as though he had destroyed the whole world. He who saves a human life is considered by Scripture as though he had preserved the whole universe (*Sanhedrin* 37a).

He who raises his hand against his neighbour, even though he did not smite him, is called a wicked man (*Sanhedrin* 58b).

Whence do we know that if a person sees his fellow-man sinking in the river or being dragged away by a wild beast, or attacked by thieves, that he is in duty bound to save him? Scripture says, *You shall not stand idly by the blood of your neighbour* (*Sanhedrin* 73a).

5 The Sanctity of Property

Next to murder, theft is one of the worst crimes against humanity. Man's life and happiness often depend on the possessions he has acquired through his industry. Not only is the thief to be punished, but also anyone who aids him in his crime, such as the receiver of stolen goods. Borrowing without intending to repay and any other wrongful taking of money or goods are equally dishonest.

Thou shalt not steal (Ex. xx, 13).

You shall not remove your neighbour's landmark (i.e. boundary-line, to enlarge your own estate) (Deut. xix, 14).

The wicked borrows but pays not (Ps. xxxvii, 21).

Let the property of your friend be as dear to you as your own (*Avoth* ii, 17).

What is yours is mine and what is mine is mine is the characteristic of a wicked person (*Avoth* v, 13).

R. Jochanan said, 'Anyone who robs his neighbour of the smallest coin is considered as though he had taken his life' (*Baba Kamma* 119a).

Not the mouse is the thief, but the hole is the thief (*Gittin* 45a).

CHAPTER 19

MAN AND HIS NEIGHBOUR

1 Honesty **2** Employer and Employee **3** Charity

1 **Honesty**

Integrity in business is one of the distinguishing marks of the upright man. The Torah places deceit, in any form, in the same category as theft. It strictly forbids cheating, advantage must not be taken in times of emergency to raise prices or give short measure. Not only is it wrong to deceive in the actual buying and selling of goods: it is equally wrong for a person to pretend he wishes to buy when, in fact, he is merely raising false hopes in the seller.

You shall not steal nor deal falsely nor lie one to another (Lev. xix, 11).

You shall do no wrong in judgment, in measures of length or weight or quantity. You shall have just balances, just weights, a just ephah and a just hin. I am the Lord your God who brought you out of the land of Egypt (Lev. xix, 35, 36).

When man is brought up for judgment in the World to Come he is first asked 'Did you deal honestly in your business transactions?' (*Shabbath* 31a).

A storekeeper must clean his measures twice a week, wipe his weights once a week and cleanse his scales after each weighing [to ensure accuracy] (*Baba Bathra* v, 10).

Of those who hoard produce (in order to corner the market and cause prices to rise) or practise usury, or give short measure, or inflate prices, Scripture says (Amos viii, 7), *The Lord has sworn by the pride of Jacob, surely I will never forget any of their deeds* (*Baba Bathra* 90b).

Just as one can wrong a person in a business transaction so can he wrong him by means of words. One must not say to another 'How much is this article?' when he has no intention of buying it (*Baba Metzia* 58b).

2 Employer and Employee

The relationship between employer and employee must be based on the principles of co-operation, trust and justice. The employer should treat his workmen fairly and pay their wages promptly; otherwise he commits an unpardonable sin. The employee, on the other hand, should devote all his time and energy to his work and carry out the instructions of his employer.

The wages of a hired servant shall not remain with you all night until the morning (Lev. xix, 13).

You shall not oppress a hired servant who is poor and needy . . . You shall give him his hire on the day he earns it, before the sun goes down (Deut. xxiv, 14, 15).

He who withholds the wages of his hired workman is considered as though he had taken his life from him (*Baba Metzia* 112a).

The workman who disregards the instructions of his employer, thereby causing him damage, is called a robber (*Baba Metzia* 78a).

A man should not work for himself by night and hire himself out during the day. He should not starve himself or inflict privation upon himself because he lessens the work of his employer thereby (*Yer. Demai* 26b).

R. Joseph had been engaged to carry out some work for a builder. Whilst standing upon some scaffolding, Oenomaus of Gadara, a heathen philosopher approached and said to him 'I have a question to ask you.' 'I cannot come down,' was the reply, 'as I am hired by the day' (Exodus *Rabbah* xiii, i).

3 Charity

The Hebrew word for charity is צְדָקָה—righteousness; when we help the poor and needy we are performing an act of righteousness and mercy. All our possessions belong to God and it is therefore our duty to help those less fortunate than ourselves to maintain their dignity and self-respect. Charity can take many forms: it includes giving and lending to the poor, and supporting the organisations which provide for their needs. The highest form of charity is that given secretly and with good grace.

You shall not harden your heart nor shut your hand from your needy brother, but you shall surely open your hand unto him and lend him sufficient for his need in that which he wants (Deut. xv, 7, 8).

Take no interest of him or increase, but fear your God, that your brother may live with you (Lev. xxv, 36).

When you reap the harvest of your land, you shall not wholly reap the corner of your field, neither shall you gather the gleaning of your harvest. And you shall not glean your vineyard, neither shall you gather the fallen fruit of your vineyard. You shall leave them for the poor and for the stranger; I am the Lord your God (Lev. xix, 9, 10).

Greater is he who does charity than all the sacrifices, as it is said (Prov. xxi, 3), *To do righteousness and justice is more acceptable to the Lord than sacrifice* (*Succah* 49b).

Give unto Him of what is His, seeing that you and what you have are His (*Avoth* iii, 8).

R. Yannai saw somebody giving a coin to a poor man in public. He said to him 'It would be preferable if you did not give anything at all rather than put him to shame' (*Chagigah* 5a).

There is another form of charity called גְּמִילוּת חֲסָדִים— 'the bestowal of loving-kindness'. It can be shown to rich and poor alike, and consists of personal attention and service to the needs of our fellow-man. Examples are:

(i) *Hospitality:* הַכְנָסַת אוֹרְחִים (lit. 'bringing in the guests'). Scripture tells how Abraham and Sarah showed hospitality towards the angels who passed by their tent. On *Seder* night we are ready to welcome any stranger to our table ('all who are in need let them come in and eat'); and it will be recalled that the Synagogue used to provide shelter for the stranger (see p. 55).

Let your house be open wide, and let the poor be the members of your household (*Avoth* i, 5).

Greater is hospitality to wayfarers than receiving the Divine Presence (*Shabbath* 127a).

Whenever Rav Huna was about to partake of a meal he opened his doors and exclaimed, 'Let anyone in need enter and eat!' (*Taanith* 20b).

(ii) *Visiting the Sick:* בִּקּוּר חוֹלִים. When we are ill we like friends to visit us and cheer us up. We feel better when we know that others are interested in our recovery. There is no direct mention of this act of benevolence in the Torah, but the Rabbis find a reference to it in the visit of God to Abraham at Mamre (Gen. xviii, 1) during his indisposition after being circumcised.

Whoever visits the sick causes him to recover (*Nedarim* 40a).

(iii) *Providing a Bride's Dowry:* הַכְנָסַת כַּלָּה . It is praiseworthy to help a young couple to get married and set up their home. Our Rabbis call it an example of 'walking humbly with your God' (*Makkoth* 24a).

(iv) *Accompanying the Dead to their Burial Place:* הַלְוָיַת הַמֵּת . This is indeed a חֶסֶד שֶׁל אֱמֶת —a true act of loving-kindness, in the words of our Rabbis, for there can be no expectation of reward. It is the highest form of respect which we can show to a fellow-man.

The study of the Torah may be suspended to carry out the dead (*Megillah* 3b).

Jacob said to Joseph, *Deal with me in kindness and truth, bury me not in Egypt* (Gen. xlvii, 29). Is there then an act of kindness which is false? But he meant 'If you carry out an act of kindness after my death, it is a kindness of truth' (*Bereshith Rabbah* xcvi, 5).

(v) *Comforting the Mourners:* נִחוּם אֲבֵלִים . This, too, say our Rabbis was one of the gracious acts of God when He blessed Isaac after the death of Abraham (Gen. xxv, 11). Sympathy and kind words help the bereaved to bear their sorrow.

CHAPTER 20

CHARACTER AND EFFORT

1 Truth **2** The Sin of Slander **3** The Pursuit of Peace
4 Humility **5** The Dignity of Labour **6** Kindness to Animals

We have discussed the teaching of Judaism on our duties to our neighbours. To fulfil them, there must be mutual trust and confidence. It is our personal character, and the esteem of others, which count in the end. *Who shall dwell upon thy holy mountain? He that walks uprightly and works righteousness and speaks truth in his heart, that has no slander upon his tongue, nor does evil to his fellow* (Ps. xv, 1 ff). Let us consider the Jewish attitude to some of the virtues and vices which establish or destroy human happiness.

1 Truth

The upright man will speak the truth in his business dealings, in his every-day conversation, and at all times. If he does otherwise he endangers the very existence of civilised society. A false word can inflict grave injury on a fellow-man. Suppressing the truth or giving a wrong impression is equally to be condemned.

You shall not deal falsely nor lie one to another (Lev. xix, 11).

Thou shalt not bear false witness against thy neighbour (Ex. xx, 13).

Keep your tongue from evil and your lips from speaking guile (Ps. xxxiv, 14).

Truth is the seal of God (*Sanhedrin* 64a).

133

With the righteous, their yea is yea and their nay is nay (*Ruth Rabbah* iii, 18).

By three things is the world preserved, by truth, by justice and by peace (*Avoth* i, 18).

God hates the person who says one thing with the mouth and another in the mind (*Pesachim* 113b).

2 The Sin of Slander

Nothing can be worse than maliciously injuring a man's good name and reputation. So grave is the sin of slander that our Rabbis equalise it with the combined sins of idolatry, immorality and bloodshed (*Yer. Peah* 16a).

You shall not utter a false report (Ex. xxiii, 1).

You shall not walk about as a talebearer among your people (Lev. xix, 16).

Whenever a person speaks slander it is as though he denied the very existence of God (*Arachin* 15b).

Slander slays three persons—the slanderer, the person to whom it is said and the person of whom it is spoken (*Arachin* 15b).

3 The Pursuit of Peace

The world's security depends on the establishment of peaceful relations between man and his neighbour. The man of peace will himself avoid arguments and quarrels, and will try to influence others to settle differences in a spirit of love and friendship. He will be a contented man and will not envy others.

Seek peace and pursue it (Ps. xxxiv, 15). i.e. seek it in your own place and pursue it elsewhere (*Yer. Peah* i, 1).

Hatred stirs up strife, but love covers all transgressions (Prov. x, 12).

The Priestly Blessing ends with the words *And may He grant you peace* (Num. vi, 26). This teaches that blessings are of no avail unless they are accompanied by peace (*Bemidbar Rabbah* xi, 17).

Be of the disciples of Aaron, loving peace and pursuing peace, loving your fellow-creatures, and bringing them near to the Torah (*Avoth* i, 12).

By establishing peace between his fellow-creatures, man will reap the benefit in this world yet the capital remains for the World to Come (see *Peah* i, 1).

Who is rich? He who is satisfied with his lot (*Avoth* iv, 1).

Thou shalt not covet thy neighbour's house . . . nor anything that is thy neighbour's (Ex. xx, 14).

4 Humility

Care must be taken not to abuse any success we may achieve in life by becoming arrogant and self-centred. The greater the man the more humble he will be, realising that his success is a gift from God to be used for the benefit of his neighbour.

The man Moses was very meek, more than any man upon the face of the earth (Num. xii, 3).

What does the Lord require of you but to do justice and to love mercy, and to walk humbly with your God (Micah vi, 8).

Whoever runs around after greatness, greatness flees from him; and whoever flees from greatness, greatness runs after him (*Eruvin* 13b).

Be humble of spirit before all men (*Avoth* iv, 12).

Humility is the greatest of all virtues (*Avodah Zarah* 20b).

Let all who occupy themselves with the community do so for the sake of heaven (and not for their own self-glory) (*Avoth* ii, 2).

5 The Dignity of Labour

The man of character will contribute to the needs of society through his physical effort and mental ability. The duty to work was one of the first which God imposed on man. *And He put him into the Garden of Eden to till it and to keep it* (Gen. ii, 15). Man was meant, through his labour, to co-operate with God in developing His Universe. Although Judaism demands that every man should study the Torah, it demands equally that he should earn a living through work. The Talmud constantly stresses the dignity of labour and the danger of idleness. Many Rabbis earned their living through a humble trade. R. Joshua was a charcoal-burner, R. Jochanan a maker of sandals, and R. Jose b. Chalafta a worker in leather.

He who is slack in his work is brother to him that is a destroyer (Prov. xviii, 9).

The study of the Torah is beneficial only when combined with some worldly occupation, for the labour demanded by both of them makes sin to be forgotten. And all study of the Torah without work must eventually become futile and lead to sin (*Avoth* ii, 2).

He who does not teach his son a trade accustoms him to robbery (*Kiddushin* 29a).

Great is work for it honours him who performs it (*Nedarim* 49b).

Idleness leads to immorality (*Kethuboth* 59b).

6 Kindness to Animals

Compassion and consideration for animals are important indications of character. Animals should be watered and fed properly and should not be overworked. They should be rested on the Sabbath, as the fourth commandment enjoins. The laws of *Shechitah*, as we have seen, are specially designed to spare the animal as much pain as possible.

You shall not muzzle the ox when he treads out the corn (Deut. xxv, 4).

You shall not plough with an ox and an ass (i.e. the stronger animal with the weaker) *together* (Deut. xxii, 10).

A man should not eat his meal before giving food to his cattle, as it is said (Deut. xi, 15) *I will give grass in your field for your cattle* and then *you shall eat and be satisfied* (*Berachoth* 40a).

None may acquire a domestic animal or wild beast or bird unless he has arranged that it be properly fed (*Yer. Yevamoth* 14d).

CHAPTER 21

THE FAMILY CIRCLE

1 The Mother 2 The Honouring of Parents 3 Education

1 **The Mother**

The woman occupies a dignified place in Jewish life for she, too, was created in God's image (Gen. i, 27) and is just as entitled as man to respect and regard. Because of her special domestic duties, the Talmud lays down a general rule that woman is exempt from all positive commandments (i.e. those which have the form of 'Thou shalt') for which a fixed time is set—מִצְוֹת עֲשֵׂה שֶׁהַזְּמַן גְרָמָא (*Kiddushin* i, 7). Women are not obliged, for instance, to dwell in the *Succah* or wear *Tzitzith* and *Tephillin*. All other positive commandments and prohibitions must be observed by women equally with men, but for a few exceptions. Members of her household should give a woman very great respect. Not only does she care for their material needs, but she is responsible for seeing that her children are educated and that her husband continues his studies.

A man should ever take especial care to pay respect to his wife. Blessing is to be found in a man's house only because of his wife, as it is said (Gen. xii, 16), *And he* (Pharaoh) *dealt well with Abram for her* (Sarah's) *sake* (*Baba Metzia* 59a).

Of him who loves his wife as himself, honours her more than himself, and trains his sons and daughters in the paths of uprightness, Scripture states (Job v, 24),

And you shall know that your tent is in peace (*Yevamoth* 62b).

Wherewith do women acquire merit? By ensuring that their children study Torah in the Synagogue and their husbands continue their higher studies in the *Beth Hamidrash* (*Berachoth* 17a).

2 The Honouring of Parents

The duty to honour parents, as laid down in the Fifth Commandment, receives special attention in Jewish literature. Both mother and father are to receive equal respect—which is placed on the same level as that accorded to God. Children should show reverence to parents by not interrupting or contradicting their opinion, by looking after them in their old age, by respecting their memory after death.

Honour thy father and thy mother that thy days may be long upon the land which the Lord thy God gives you (Ex. xx, 12).

You shall fear every man his mother and his father (Lev. xix, 3).

Man has three partners: God, his father and mother. When a man honours his father and mother, God says, 'I consider this as though I myself lived among them and honour was paid to me' (*Kiddushin* 30b).

What is meant by fear and by honour? Fear means that the son does not stand or sit in his father's place, nor does he contradict his words or decide against his opinions. Honour means that he provides him with food and drink, clothing him and caring for him (*Kiddushin* 31b).

A man should honour his parents both during their lives and after their death (*Kiddushin* 31b).

3 Education

It has always been the father's chief duty 'to teach them [the Commandments] diligently to his children' (Deut. vi, 7) and to encourage a love for learning for its own sake. If the father was unable to teach his child, either because he lacked the knowledge, or could not spare the time from his own studies, a private teacher was engaged or the child was sent to the Jewish school. The Jews' great passion for education lead to the setting up of higher schools for youths by Simeon ben Shatach in the first century B.C.E. Elementary schools for boys were founded in Palestine by Joshua ben Gamala in the first century C.E. and the Rabbis developed an educational system throughout the country, providing for elementary, adolescent and adult studies.

In early times girls had been trained in domestic duties at home; they were not admitted to the schools, but some of them were given a private education by their parents at home, and there are several cases of women learned in the Torah, like Beruriah, the wife of R. Meir. In later centuries, however, facilities were gradually increased for girls to receive at least elementary instruction in Hebrew reading and translation. Nowadays, girls are able to pursue their Jewish and Hebrew studies without restriction.

Whoever has a son occupying himself in the study of the Torah is as though he never dies (*Bereshith Rabbah* xlix, 4).

The world exists only through the breath of school-children . . . The instruction of children may not be interrupted even for the rebuilding of the Temple . . . A city in which there are no school children will suffer destruction (*Shabbath* 119b).

He who learns as a child, to what can he be likened?

To ink written on new paper. But he who learns as an old man, to what can he be likened? To ink written on blotted paper (*Avoth* iv, 25).

If you have acquired knowledge, what do you lack? If you lack knowledge, what have you acquired? (*Vayikra Rabbah* i, 6).

Children were expected to pay even greater respect to teachers than to parents. Teachers were considered by our Rabbis to be guardians of the citadel of Judaism, 'turning many to righteousness'.

The parent brings the child to the life of this world, but the teacher brings him to the life of the world to come (*Baba Metzia* ii, 11).

They that turn many to righteousness are like the stars for ever and ever (Dan. xii, 3). This applies to the teachers of children (*Baba Bathra* 8b).

Let the honour of your pupil be as dear as your own, and the honour of your fellow-student as the reverence for your teacher, and the reverence for your teacher as the fear of Heaven (*Avoth* iv, 15).

A GLANCE AT THE FUTURE

We must often think: how much happier the world would be if the human race carried out the principles of life and conduct set out in the preceding pages! Unhappily we are still far from realising the mission for which Israel was selected to serve humanity. Universal peace, the belief in One God and the Brotherhood of Man would then become accomplished facts. The Jewish people have never been deterred from continuing their efforts towards this goal, encouraged by the teachings of their faith and inspired by the belief in the Messiah and the Messianic age.

1 The Golden Age of the Messiah

The Hebrew word מָשִׁיחַ—Messiah—means 'anointed.' It is applied, in the Bible, to a king and the High Priest, who were anointed with oil when about to ascend the throne or assume office. Whenever our prophets and teachers speak of the Messiah they stress that he will be a *human* being chosen by God, endowed with exceptional qualities, and divinely inspired to carry out his task.

The Messiah's arrival, say our prophets, will bring about (*a*) the triumph of righteousness over evil, (*b*) the restoration of scattered Israel to the Holy Land, and (*c*) the peace of all mankind who will acknowledge the supremacy of One God. Such is the inspiring message of Isaiah.

In Chapter XI of his book he says that the Redeemer would be a descendant of the house of Jesse, the father of David, upon whom will rest the *spirit of knowledge and of the fear of the Lord*. He will destroy wickedness, *and righteousness shall be the girdle of his loins*. Isaiah depicts the Golden Age of Peace when even *the wolf shall dwell with the lamb . . . and the earth shall be full of the knowledge of the Lord as the waters cover the sea*. On that day the Messiah *will assemble the dispersed of Israel, and gather together the scattered of Judah from the four corners of the earth.*

The ideal world is called by our Rabbis 'the Kingdom of God'—מַלְכוּת שַׁדַּי. The Holy Land will form its central inspiration. It is best described by quoting the famous words of Isaiah and Micah (Isaiah ii, 2-4; Micah iv, 1-4): *And it shall come to pass in the end of days, that the Lord's House shall be established on the top of the mountains and shall be exalted above the hills, and all nations shall flow unto it. And many people shall go and say, Come let us go up to the mountain of the Lord, to the House of the God of Jacob; and He will teach us of His ways and we will walk in His paths; for out of Zion will go forth the law and the word of the Lord from Jerusalem. And He shall judge between the nations and shall decide for many peoples; and they shall beat their swords into ploughshares and their spears into pruning-hooks; nations shall not lift up sword against nation, neither shall they learn war any more.*

Some Jewish thinkers do not insist on a personal Messiah but lay greater emphasis on the conception of a Messianic Age. The universal rule of righteousness, they maintain, will be brought about by the combined efforts of all men, with God as their guiding power. This view does not affect the essential belief in the ultimate redemption of Israel and of mankind. Faith in the coming of the

Messianic Age has given comfort and encouragement to the Jewish people especially in times of persecution. In spite of their many tragic experiences, they do not despair that the time will come when 'the Lord shall be King over all the earth; in that day the Lord shall be One and His name One.'

2 The Resurrection of the Dead: תְּחִיַת הַמֵּתִים

Judaism teaches that after man's death the soul returns to God who gave it, and in the World to Come the righteous will be rewarded and the wicked punished. The Rabbis held that the resurrection of the dead will take place after the Messiah has appeared. Among those who have no share in the World to Come, the Rabbis declared, is the person who denies the belief in this principle of faith (*Sanhedrin* x, 1). Dealing elsewhere with this question, they make it clear that this reward in the World to Come would be granted only to those who deserve it, emphasizing once again the importance of leading a righteous life in this world. Jewish philosophers have tried to indicate the form the Resurrection will take, but the truth of the matter is: this is beyond our limited knowledge and experience. So firmly have we clung to this belief in the Resurrection that we proclaim it daily in our *Amidah* prayer.

APPENDIX

1 The Ten Commandments

In Temple times, the Ten Commandments were among the Blessings and Scriptural passages recited when the morning sacrifice was being offered (*Tamid* v, 1). Our *Siddur*, therefore, includes the Decalogue among the additional sections to the *Shacharith* Service. The first five Commandments, engraved on the first Tablet of Stone given to Moses on Mount Sinai, deal with the duties of man towards God—בֵּין אָדָם לַמָּקוֹם; the second five deal with the duties of man towards his neighbour—בֵּין אָדָם לַחֲבֵרוֹ.

1 I am the Lord thy God who brought thee out of the land of Egypt, out of the house of bondage.

2 Thou shalt have no other gods before me. Thou shalt not make unto thee a graven image; nor the form of anything that is in heaven above, or that is in the earth beneath, or that is in the water under the earth; thou shalt not bow down thyself unto them, nor serve them; for I the Lord thy God am a jealous God, visiting the iniquity of the fathers upon the children, upon the third and upon the fourth generation, unto them that hate me: and showing loving-kindness to the thousandth generation, unto them that love me and keep my commandments.

3 Thou shalt not take the name of the Lord thy God in vain; for the Lord will not hold him guiltless that taketh his name in vain.

4 Remember the sabbath day to keep it holy. Six days shalt thou labour, and do all thy work; but the seventh

day is a sabbath onto the Lord thy God: in it thou shalt not do any work, thou, nor thy son, nor thy daughter, thy manservant, nor thy maidservant, nor thy cattle, nor the stranger that is within thy gates: for in six days the Lord made heaven and earth, the sea and all that is therein, and rested on the seventh day: wherefore the Lord blessed the sabbath day and hallowed it.

5 Honour thy father and thy mother: that thy days may be long upon the land which the Lord thy God giveth thee.

6 Thou shalt not murder.

7 Thou shalt not commit adultery.

8 Thou shalt not steal.

9 Thou shalt not bear false witness against thy neighbour.

10 Thou shalt not covet thy neighbour's house, thou shalt not covet thy neighbour's wife, nor his manservant, nor his maidservant, nor his ox, nor his ass, nor anything that is thy neighbour's.

2 The Thirteen Principles of Faith

The שְׁלֹשָׁה עָשָׂר עִקָּרִים—the Thirteen Principles of Faith—included in our *Siddur*—are based on the teachings of Maimonides in his Arabic commentary on the Mishnah to Tractate *Sanhedrin*. Though, in later years, many religious thinkers disagreed with his views, the Thirteen Principles have remained the most popular presentation of the basic beliefs of Judaism. The *Yigdal* poem also takes them as its theme, each of the thirteen lines summarizing one of the Principles.

1 I believe with perfect faith that the Creator, blessed be His name, is the Author and Guide of everything that has been created, and that He alone has made, does make, and will make all things.

2 I believe with perfect faith that the Creator, Blessed be His name, is a Unity, and that there is no unity in any manner like unto His, and that He alone is our God, who was, is, and will be.

3 I believe with perfect faith that the Creator, blessed be His name, is not a body, and that He is free from all the accidents of matter, and that He has not any form whatsoever.

4 I believe with perfect faith that the Creator, blessed be His name, is the first and the last.

5 I believe with perfect faith that to the Creator, blessed be His name, and to Him alone it is right to pray, and that it is not right to pray to any being besides Him.

6 I believe with perfect faith that all the words of the prophets are true.

7 I believe with perfect faith that the prophecy of Moses our teacher, peace be unto him, was true, and that he was the chief of the prophets, both of those that preceded and of those that followed him.

8 I believe with perfect faith that the whole Law, now in our possession, is the same that was given to Moses our teacher, peace be unto him.

9 I believe with perfect faith that this Law will not be changed, and that there will never be any other law from the Creator, blessed be His name.

10 I believe with perfect faith that the Creator, blessed be His name, knows every deed of the children of men, and all their thoughts, as it is said, *It is He that fashioneth the hearts of them all, that giveth heed to all their deeds* (Ps. xxxiii, 15).

11 I believe with perfect faith that the Creator, blessed be His name, rewards those that keep His commandments, and punishes those that transgress them.

12 I believe with perfect faith in the coming of the

Messiah, and, though he tarry, I will wait daily for his coming.

13 I believe with perfect faith that there will be a resurrection of the dead at the time when it shall please the Creator, blessed be His name, and exalted be the remembrance of Him for ever and ever.

3 The Jewish Calendar

1 Nisan: נִיסָן

	שַׁבַּת הַגָּדוֹל—the Great Sabbath, the Sabbath before Passover (p. 101).
14th	תַּעֲנִית בְּכוֹרִים—the Fast of the First-born (p. 62).
15th to 22nd	פֶּסַח—Passover (p. 62). Also called
	חַג הַמַּצּוֹת—the Festival of Unleavened Bread (p. 62); and
	זְמַן חֲרוּתֵנוּ—the Season of our Freedom (p. 63).
16th	סְפִירַת הָעֹמֶר—the Counting of the *Omer* begins (p. 69).
17th to 20th	חוֹל הַמּוֹעֵד—the 'secular' days of the Festival (p. 61).
23rd	אִסְרוּ חַג—the day after the Festival (p. 61).

2 Iyyar: אִייָר

5th	יוֹם הָעַצְמָאוּת—Independence Day (p.92).
	שֵׁנִי חֲמִישִׁי וְשֵׁנִי—the fast days observed by some on a Monday, Thursday and following Monday (p 97).
14th	פֶּסַח שֵׁנִי—the second Passover (p. 70).
18th	ל״ג בָּעֹמֶר—the thirty-third day of the *Omer*; the Scholar's Feast (p. 69).

3 Sivan: סִיוָן

3rd to 5th שְׁלֹשֶׁת יְמֵי הַגְבָּלָה—the three days of bordering (p. 73).

6th & 7th שָׁבוּעוֹת—the Feast of Weeks (p. 71). Also called

חַג הַקָּצִיר—the Festival of the Wheat Harvest (p. 71);

יוֹם הַבִּכּוּרִים—the Day of the First-fruits (p. 71);

זְמַן מַתַּן תּוֹרָתֵנוּ—the Season of the Giving of our Law (p. 72); and

עֲצֶרֶת—'concluding' Festival (p. 72).

8th אִסְרוּ חַג—the day after the Festival (p. 61).

4 Tammuz: תַּמּוּז

17th שִׁבְעָה עָשָׂר בְּתַמּוּז—the fast of the 17th of *Tammuz* (p. 94).

5 Av: אָב

שַׁבָּת חָזוֹן—the Sabbath of 'Vision,' the Sabbath before the 9th of *Av* (p. 102).

9th תִּשְׁעָה בְּאָב—the fast of the 9th of *Av* (p. 95).

שַׁבָּת נַחֲמוּ—the Sabbath of 'Comfort Ye', the Sabbath after the 9th of *Av* (p. 102).

15th חֲמִשָּׁה עָשָׂר בְּאָב—celebration of the wood-offering on the 15th of *Av* (p. 91).

6 Elul: אֱלוּל

the month of preparation for the Solemn Days (p. 79).

7 Tishri: תִּשְׁרִי

1st to 10th עֲצֶרֶת יְמֵי תְשׁוּבָה—the ten days of repentance (p. 78).

1st & 2nd רֹאשׁ הַשָּׁנָה—the New Year (p. 79). Also

Tishri—*continued*

	יוֹם תְּרוּעָה—called the day of sounding the *shophar* (p. 79);
	זִכְרוֹן תְּרוּעָה—the memorial of the sounding of the *shophar* (p. 79);
	יוֹם הַזִּכָּרוֹן—the day of Memorial (p. 80); and
	יוֹם הַדִּין—the day of Judgment (p. 80).
3rd	צוֹם גְּדַלְיָה—the fast of Gedaliah (p. 95).
10th	יוֹם כִּפּוּר—the Day of Atonement (p. 83).
15th to 21st	סֻכּוֹת—the Festival of Tabernacles (p. 73). Also called
	חַג הָאָסִיף—the Festival of Ingathering (p. 74);
	זְמַן שִׂמְחָתֵנוּ—the Season of our Rejoicing (p. 75); and
	חַג—Festival (p. 74).
17th to 21st	חוֹל הַמּוֹעֵד—the 'secular' days of the Festival (p. 61).
21st	הוֹשַׁעְנָא רַבָּא—the 'great Hoshana' Service (p. 75).
22nd & 23rd	שְׁמִינִי עֲצֶרֶת—the eighth day of Solemn Assembly (p. 76).
23rd	שִׂמְחַת תּוֹרָה—Rejoicing of the Law (p. 76).
24th	אִסְרוּ חַג—the day after the Festival (p. 61).

8 Marcheshvan: מַרְחֶשְׁוָן

| | שֵׁנִי, חֲמִישִׁי וְשֵׁנִי—the fast days observed by some on a Monday, Thursday and following Monday (p. 97). |

9 Kislev: כִּסְלֵו

| 25th to 2nd or 3rd of *Teveth* | חֲנֻכָּה—Feast of Re-dedication (p. 86). |

10 Teveth: טֵבֵת

עֲשָׂרָה בְּטֵבֵת—the fast of the 10th of *Teveth*. (p. 94).

11 Shevat: שְׁבָט

15th   ראש הַשָּׁנָה לָאִילָנוֹת—the New Year for trees (p. 91).

שַׁבָּת שְׁקָלִים—the Sabbath relating to Shekels, the Sabbath before or on the 1st of *Adar* (p. 99).

12 Adar: אֲדָר

שַׁבָּת זָכוֹר—the Sabbath of 'Remember,' the Sabbath before *Purim* (p. 100).

13th   תַּעֲנִית אֶסְתֵּר—the Fast of Esther (p. 89).

14th   פּוּרִים—the Feast of Lots (p. 88).

15th   שׁוּשַׁן פּוּרִים—Shushan *Purim* (p. 90).

שַׁבָּת פָּרָה—the Sabbath of the (Red) Heifer, the first or second Sabbath after *Purim* (p. 100).

שַׁבָּת הַחֹדֶשׁ—the Sabbath of the month (of *Nisan*), the Sabbath before or on the 1st of *Nisan* (p. 101).

In a leap year all these occasions are observed in *Adar Sheni*; and *Shabbath Shekalim* then falls on the Sabbath before or on the 1st of *Adar Sheni*.

4 Glossary of Hebrew Terms

153

GLOSSARY OF HEBREW TERMS

GLOSSARY OF HEBREW TERMS

5 General Index